Relationship Magic
The Secret to Happily Ever After

For information contact:
Destiny Publications
P.O.Box 1011
New Canaan, CT 06840

Book production by: The Cadence Group
Edited by: Lesley Bolton
Interior design and layout by 1106 Design
Cover design by: Gwyn Kennedy Snider
Title page composition by: Jayne Richards

ISBN 13 – 978-0-9794901-0-1
ISBN 10 – 0-9794901-0-3

Library of Congress Control Number: 2007935064

Printed in Canada

Praise for Dr. Edythe Denkin:

"A refreshing and unique "How-To-Book...charming!"
— Jane Powell, actress

"An interesting and novel approach to an important subject — the reconnecting of partners to create an enduring relationship."
— Marsha Temlock, Author, "Your Child's Divorce (What You Can Do)"

"Dr. Denkin developed a formula to help you enjoy the magical moments, and to feel happy to do the work creating them."
— Ginny Pangallo, Intuitive Coach

"She is a combination of that friend who always seems to know how to make you feel better, a consummate professional and the type of Jewish mother we all should have had."
— New Canaan Advertiser

Dear Edythe, I have completed my first reading of "Why Can't You Catch Me Being Good?" I loved it. I mailed off a copy to the parents of my grandchild, and purchased a copy for my elder brother, and recommended it to my Wednesday night "Keeping the Love You Find" group, and recommended it to several of my clients as a re-parenting book and wrote it up in my church book review. Thank you for your shared wisdom.

Respectfully yours,
Shauna Jean Stott, Ph.D.,
Clinical Psychologist

Acknowledgments

Thank you to my husband (my James) for your patience, understanding, and support. It is my hope that the work we are constantly doing to keep ourselves and our love growing will be an example our children can follow and profit from.

And thank you to my three sons for your constant support, and to my daughters-in-law Jenni for your excellent suggestions and superb editing and Wonah for being there for me at the inception. Thank you to Woody, my new-age designer dog—half Bischon and half Yorkie—for your truly accurate part in the story, and to Bridgett, your mother, who helped raise you.

Many thanks also goes to you, David Laxer, an amazing Buddhist Monk, as you were instrumental in bringing the knowledge of Buddhism into this work; Ginny Pangallo, who was with me every step of the way with inspiration and spiritual guidance always when needed; Rene Avery, who also gave me guided inspiration throughout this work; Stirling Davenport, my first editor; Howie Sanns, who offered editorial advice; Virginia Gentry, who continues to provide support and encouragement; and Sheila Pakula, who was there in the beginning with needed writing assistance. Thank you, Lesley Bolton for being such a wonderful editor and Amy Collins, my publishing consultant, for all of your help.

Satori is a role model for both male and female to tract a new way of being where you do not have to live with anger or hostility.

There are people who allow anger to guide their decisions, and if they want to live like that, let them. It is their choice of how they want to live—just a different path. Look down that path and see where it will end— usually in misery, sickness, or both.

You cannot expect your life to work just because of James and Cinda, but you can learn a different path— and find a Satori who can help you.

—DAVID LAXER, BUDDHIST MONK

Preface

$\mathcal{R}$*elationship Magic* is an active learning experience, showing you through self-realization how to keep the magic alive in your relationship. The story has intentionally been put into the form of a fairytale in order to help you identify your own thoughts, feelings, and behaviors. The main characters, James and Cinda, embark on a journey of healing and growth with the benevolent guidance of their wise mentor, Satori.

Through active participation, you will feel your emotions and allow them to flow without criticism or judgment of yourself or your partner. Use your imagination and senses to experience the characters within you and to identify your unconscious reactions.

Becoming aware of unconscious reactions and summoning the courage to change them is a struggle that many couples face. Doing so can literally breathe new life into a relationship. You will see how understanding the reasons behind your reactions can help you in your marriage. Just as for James and Cinda, it will not be an easy task for you. Although it involves pain and requires perseverance, it is the most worthwhile journey you can pursue. It is through this process that you become the real you.

You will find that, as is the situation with most couples, James and Cinda have similar childhood wounds but handle them in opposite ways. This serves as the basis for their unconscious attraction to each other. Through the wisdom and guidance of their mentor, Satori, this troubled couple is led from the brink of divorce to a deep and lasting relationship. If you discover similarities between your relationship and that of James and Cinda, you are encouraged to seek a Satori, or a wise therapist, to help you along your way towards relationship magic.

Introduction

*R*elationship *Magic* has been written as a tribute to Imago Relationship Therapy and Harville Hendrix, its founder. The genius of Imago Relationship Therapy is acquiring the ability to not take what is said or done personally through developing the skills needed for intentional dialogue.

While each of us wants to feel like a prince or princess, we cannot do so without developing the necessary skills to find gratitude within and the ability to recognize the magical moments in our relationships. This is difficult, indeed, as we all must live in the reality of every day.

Intentional dialogue is the tool that Harville Hendrix brought to marriage and is what brings relationship magic into our lives. After twenty-five years of experience in Imago, I have seen many couples that have acquired the ability to dialogue and empathize with their partner's point of view—but rarely do so. They say, "It is not natural," "People don't talk that way," "It takes too long to talk that way," "You cannot really express yourself," etc. So instead, they continue to argue and feel frustrated and unloved by talking in the same manner they learned as children. No wonder they believe they have lost the magic.

The sacred truth is that although each of us dreams like a prince or princess, we find that we have to live in our daily reality. And when we are not doing the work in the marriage, the kingdom is not magical. Although the secret to happiness is to enjoy the moments, we also must want to feel happy to do the work creating them.

Cinda and James's fairytale is representative of typical events in the lives of the hundreds of couples I have helped over the past twenty-five years. In the beginning, when their relationship brings them so many magical moments, they look forward to spending the rest of their lives together, and they commit to marriage. But after the first few years, the same criticism, blame, and shame they absorbed from their parents begins to creep into their lives. Because they unknowingly bring the same negative energy of their childhood wounds into their marriage, they find they are repeating similar patterns of their parents that they swore they would never do.

Luckily for them, they find Satori with whom to study and learn. He teaches them their most valuable lesson: developing the skill of intentional dialogue. From this experience, they develop the ability to not take what the other says personally. You see, Satori teaches them that when they are criticized or blamed, they are brought back to their childhood where all they wanted was to please mommy or daddy but found they could not do so. By dialoguing with their chosen partner today, they become aware that they are not children anymore and learn how to stop taking what happens personally. Instead, they learn that what is said is not about them.

Readers watch as James's and Cinda's adult realizations free them from being victims and allow them to feel and enjoy the many new moments each day brings. Therefore, our tale teaches readers how to empower themselves. They watch as Cinda and James develop consciousness of the daily signs in their lives, and by so doing, their newly developed awareness brings them to learning how to not repeat what happened when they were children. Cinda's and James's knowledge helps them use the bad that happens to create good moments, rather than become victims of each other.

Enjoy, also, reading about Woodrow, Satori's friend and companion. This little dog is the model of what every relationship needs to thrive and grow: unconditional love and acceptance. Woodrow interacts with and teaches James and Cinda how to love without criticism or blame.

In the end, you too can receive the unconditional love and acceptance that you have craved all of your life but could not get as a child. And you too will learn how intentional dialogue can become your best friend and trusted adviser.

1

A Marriage in Peril

*O*nce upon a time in the faraway kingdom of Lavonia, there lived a young prince named James. Prince James was kind and generous. He showed great promise as a future ruler of the kingdom. The royal family lived in splendor in a beautiful castle. The lavish balls and ceremonies of state were a continued source of admiration and wonder for the citizens of the kingdom and visiting dignitaries. Prince James received the best education and all the material wealth that befit a young prince. He grew tall and strong. The citizens of Lavonia felt secure in the future of their monarchy.

However, as is often the case, behind the castle walls, all was not well within the royal household. The king and queen, once the happiest of lovers, had begun to grow apart not long after young James was born. The volatile King John often reacted to his queen with unrelenting and thoughtless criticism. The queen abhorred confrontation and simply walked away when the king was in one of his

1

tempers. This practice continued until the royal couple became so distant that they were almost strangers.

Young James did not escape his father's wrath. He himself was often a target. Taking after his mother, Prince James did not quarrel with his father. He attempted to avoid confrontation by putting distance between himself and the king and nurturing his dreams for the future. He longed for the day when he would meet his soul mate and find all the love and affection he craved but could not find within his own family.

Many miles away, there lived a beautiful young maiden named Cinda. She, too, longed for escape from her family turmoil. Her parents, also once so happy and in love, had fallen on hard times. Her mother could find no good in her father. As he was a weak man, and could not face his wife, he decided to seek his fortune and happiness elsewhere, leaving young Cinda and her mother to fend for themselves. Cinda's mother, in her despair, became bitter and angry, and poor Cinda often felt the lash of her sharp tongue. The desolate young girl would stare out her window, dreaming of her prince, her knight in shining armor who would rescue her, shower her with love and attention, and most importantly, never leave her.

One day, as Prince James was on a mission for his father, he encountered Cinda, who was on an errand for her mother. It was love at first sight. The young couple soon fell to planning their wedding. Their minds and hearts filled with love and hope for a bright and happy future.

The royal wedding, lavish and extravagant, lifted the hearts of the hopeful nation. As they were joined together in a wedding fit for a king and queen, Cinda and James in all their happiness could not foresee that they had embarked on a difficult and perilous journey that all soul mates must undertake if they wish to find one another and grow together.

Most fairytales end here, with the wedding and the deceptively simple "happily ever after," but as those of us in reality know, the adventure is just beginning, and so it is for Cinda and James. For a while, all appears well in the royal marriage. Cinda and James show all the signs of being deeply in love. Soon, they produce two lovely children, Lucinda and Luke. The young couple shares their hopes and dreams, their trials and disappointments. There doesn't seem to be enough hours in the day to say all that they wish to say.

However, gradually, the royal couple starts to drift apart, as their parents did. It appears that the scars of their childhoods are haunting them still. James and Cinda watch with growing frustration as their relationship unravels and the bond between them weakens.

Now, several years after that happy and wondrous wedding day, Prince James, once the most eligible and charming bachelor his kingdom has ever known, awakens in the early morning from a restless sleep. His wife, Princess Cinda, lies asleep next to him, her blond hair furled out upon the satin pillow and a slight frown on her face.

James peers out the windows of his beautiful castle at the magnificent sunrise. His eyes take in a scene of captivating beauty and peace. Yet he is deeply distressed. He is deeply grieved over the disintegration of his marriage and he feels helpless to change the course of his relationship.

James kneels to pray. He remembers his wedding day, his happiest day, when he was filled with hope for a bright future for himself and his kingdom. Cinda stood beside him, the most beautiful of princesses. All the people, noble and common, celebrated their union and shared their optimism. He bows his head and quietly prays, pouring out his hurt and disillusionment. "Dear God, although I know deeply within that you have not deserted me, I cannot understand what has happened to my life. It has been just seven years since the kingdom celebrated our wedding, the happiest of my days. Where has our happiness gone? Our marriage lifted the hearts of the people I so dearly love. Father and Mother beamed with pride at Cinda, my lovely bride, and me. Now, I am afraid we will lose it all."

Meanwhile, Cinda, now awake, lies motionless in the bed. She too feels the strain in their marriage. This morning, as most mornings, confused and frustrated thoughts about the state of her relationship swirl around in her mind. *I feel as though James and I no longer know each other. We were so close, but now, we barely speak to each other.* As she continues to ponder the dreadful turn their relationship has taken, her eyes fill with tears at a feeling of hopelessness that threatens to engulf her. *I miss him,* she thinks. *He seems so far from me now.*

Questions:
When did disillusionment mar your relationship dreams?

What did you do about it?

2

The Wise Sage, Satori

*F*ar away, outside a small, unobtrusive cottage, a tall man with deep brown eyes and a flowing white beard sits outside meditating amidst the sights and sounds of nature at its most beautiful. The simple cottage that is his home contains only a few basic necessities, mostly home-made. Two tall, carved wooden chairs for his rare guests and a simple table stand in the center of the room. A slab of wood for a bed with one small pillow and blanket is tucked neatly in the corner by his well-tended fireplace. Two luxurious crimson velvet cushions lay on the floor, gifts from a former wealthy and grateful student.

A modest and humble man, Satori revels in the captivating beauty and magnificence of the mountains. Lacking in material possessions but surrounded by the beauty of nature, he is endowed with the wealth of peace and happiness.

A small blond dog stands at his side. His silky hair shines in the early morning light, and his warm brown eyes are filled with intelligence and understanding.

Satori and his fellow sages work tirelessly to develop and share their powers and knowledge with humankind. For many centuries, Satori has studied the intricacies of human relationships and has used his accumulated wisdom to guide and assist couples whose relationships are in danger of breaking down. Many troubled couples came to study with him in his mountain retreat, gratefully trying to absorb the wisdom he offered. However, in spite of his high hopes, he disappointedly watched as the success each couple worked so diligently to achieve lasted but a fleeting moment. Instead of enlightenment, he saw looks of hopelessness and frustration on the faces of those who had set out with such expectation.

Above all, Satori desires to find a way to help humans maintain the ways of peace. In his experience, however, it seems that few couples are willing and determined enough to do the work necessary to keep their relationships strong and growing. They fail to understand that relationships are like gardens; they need daily tending and weeding. He continues in his determination to find the magic words that will teach the couples that they must nourish themselves before they can nourish their partners.

Unbeknownst to Prince James and Princess Cinda, Satori has been sent by the gods to help the future king and queen of Lavonia, whose marriage is of great importance to the well-being and security of their small kingdom. He watches them from afar through a mirror in his magic dwelling in the mountains. He sees the signs of impending trouble emerge early on in the marriage and watches as these problems continue to grow and create a wedge between the prince and princess. He has seen this happen before, and he knows that without assistance, both the prince and princess will continue to grow more and more bitter, and the kingdom will suffer.

The royal couple struggle with wounds from their pasts. Prince James has always craved respect and love from his father, which he felt he never received. He sees much in Cinda's behavior that is similar to his father's. Cinda perceives the same negativity in James that she felt in her mother, and because she did not learn to trust her mother as a child, she now is unable to trust James. The universe brought the two together in marriage to grow. Satori knows that, therefore, some pain will be necessary. James's and Cinda's parents were cowards in their marriages. The question now is whether James and Cinda will be also.

The prince and princess are both suffering from childhood wounds, unintentionally inflicted on them by their parents' criticism and abandonment. The unconscious repetition of parental behaviors each learned are what initially attracted them to each other. The unfortunate

> **What do I find in myself that I dislike so much which causes me to condemn it in my partner?**

couple is learning that a life of material abundance in the royal palace alone does not offer lasting happiness. Romantic love has faded, as it inevitably does, and they are in the next stage of marriage—realization. The couple desperately needs to learn self-awareness to deepen their love and save their crumbling marriage.

In spite of their present difficulties, Satori sees greatness in them. He has faith in their ability to lead the tiny kingdom to a bright future. But before they can inspire and wisely rule their kingdom, they must first repair and strengthen their fractured relationship. If they can replace the negative traits they learned from their parents with positive traits of their own, they will thrive. Satori longs to guide Prince James and Princess Cinda to create and rule a new kind of kingdom—one that does away with blame, shame, criticism, and deceit, filled with couples who desire to learn how to keep the magic in their relationships. For a kingdom of happy families is a kingdom of strength and prosperity. He has had to wait for this time to begin his work as he sees that people are now ready to leave their misery behind and are searching for a new, more fulfilling way to live. It is Satori's destiny to help Princess Cinda and Prince James and their marriage thrive rather than break apart through lack of communication and deceit.

> **For you only have the power to change yourself, not the other. Self-awareness and self-forgiveness are the tools needed to lead a more fulfilling way of life.**

James and Cinda must learn that rather than blame the other, it is imperative for them to ask themselves what they find in themselves that they dislike in their partners. Satori must teach them that the key to self-empowerment is learning to love themselves. When they have become empowered, they will develop the confidence to assess how their own behavior evokes reactions in their partners. In this way, they can keep their marriage from disintegrating into bitterness and hate and learn the secret language of lasting love.

Satori is eager to begin to help the couple heal. The welfare of the kingdom is directly linked to the health of the prince and princess's relationship. However, Satori cannot help until the royal couple asks him. Only when they recognize their need for guidance can he go to them. And so, he waits.

***

Questions:

What are the positive and negative traits of your parents?

Which traits do you find in your partner?

As the answers reveal themselves, you will already be finding a clue to why you react strongly to each other in certain instances.

***

3

James Recognizes His Need

$\mathscr{A}$s he contemplates the state of his marriage and what to do about it, James remembers how proud and fortunate he felt in the beginning of their marriage. He considered himself blessed in every way. He vowed to give his princess whatever she desired to make up for her lonely childhood and to protect her from stress and worry. With his beautiful princess at his side, James dreamed of greatness for his kingdom and marriage. He planned to build a kingdom in which the people had work, prosperity, and security, a kingdom in which all people would feel as blessed as he did then. He promised himself he would be a different king from his father, whom he believed to be a deeply unhappy man. James decided he would be a good husband and father, unlike King John.

Now, seven years into his marriage, Prince James has reached the point of desperation. He wonders how it could all have gone so wrong. He indulges Cinda's every whim and gives her whatever she wants. James's desire to protect her from stress and worry has led him to jeopardize his kingdom's financial security. James does not realize the folly of this way of thinking. He is completely unable to tell Cinda his true feelings, and he avoids expressing his feelings for fear of her reaction.

He cannot know that she reacts the way she does because she fears abandonment above all. She has no positive modeling upon which to base a healthy marriage. Her mother's bitter complaints about her father have taught Cinda that men are not to be trusted.

Cinda's artistic talents are well-known and admired throughout the kingdom. She has applied these skills with great fervor to the redecoration of the castle. While James admires her work, he worries about the cost. He has not discussed the budget with her, and Princess Cinda spends extravagantly, unaware of the harm she may be doing. James had told Cinda, "Your wish is my command." She has taken it literally. James now does not know how to extricate himself from this rash declaration and fears her reaction if he should attempt to curb her spending. He naively believes that Cinda knows how to build a marriage and a reign that will endure. However, Cinda had only her mother and no model of a healthy marriage, or even an unhealthy one as James had.

Satori waits in his mountain retreat for Prince James to call for help. He has studied their relationship and can see that what Cinda really needs is emotional support. That and not endless material acquisitions will help her find her own inner security. James must learn that he is not responsible for Cinda's happiness. He must also address his own suspicions about Cinda's real intentions. Satori has seen the same problems arise in many couples of all levels of wealth and society.

Satori watches in his magic mirror as James reaches a conclusion. He decides that he will seek help wherever it may be. He recognizes that the responsibilities of being a great king, husband, and father are too great to handle alone. James sighs, relief beginning to relax the tense-ness of his features. He has recognized that there are problems he cannot face alone and is now determined to find a solution.

James has taken the first step. Satori prepares to give James a sign that help is near.

Questions:

Do you feel responsible for your partner's happiness?

What negative beliefs do you have about your partner's personality and behaviors?

4

The Romantic Phase of Marriage

*T*hat evening, sleep does not come to James. In order to soothe himself, he thinks about the beginning, when he and Cinda were living their dream and were still captivated by the distractions of a new marriage. They enjoyed the simple pleasures of every touch, every look, every caress, as they uncovered the secrets within each other's bodies. After lovemaking, they remained close, sharing trust, interdependence, and dreams of their children to come.

Cinda tosses uncomfortably, also unable to sleep. To ease the tension, her mind wanders back to the day James asked her to pack her bags and, without telling her why, whisked her off to a private island they had longed to see. The sun, the wind, the warmth, James's loving touches, and the ninety-foot yacht on which they traveled were beyond even Cinda's expectations. Enchanted by James's romantic surprises, especially this one, Cinda truly felt loved and cherished for the first time in her life.

When James came home after an aggravating day of business for the king, Cinda herself prepared James's favorite meal. James was charmed that Cinda chose to cook for him, while Gilsa, her servant, stood in waiting. And Cinda herself was most pleased with her accomplishment.

Cinda would send for exotic clothes from abroad in colors that brought out James's deep brown eyes. James gave Cinda silk gowns and precious gems just to see her smile. Before he returned from travel on business, a dozen bright red roses would be waiting to greet Cinda. On the days when he felt tense, tired, or frustrated, Cinda arranged a massage for him with exotic oils to raise his spirits. She listened intently as he spoke of what ailed him.

James told many stories about the king, while Cinda openly shared tales of her childhood, each receiving support from the other. They spoke often of their dreams: James wanted to build an ideal kingdom; Cinda aspired to be an artist, bringing elegance and beauty everywhere. Their rare fights quickly dissipated into preferred lovemaking, as both felt very contented and happy during their first year of marriage.

In the beginning, their strong attraction towards each other was based on the more superficial traits of looks, charm, and material wealth. As James gave Cinda the material gifts she never received as a child, she felt a temporary but powerful security. The problems arose as Cinda believed that she would continue to get whatever she asked for, no matter how difficult to obtain, and James naively believed that he could continue to give Cinda material gifts unconditionally without building resentment towards her.

Cinda admired James in every way, as she viewed him through a romantic haze. She believed that all James needed was for her to be there to hold his hand. It was during those moments, when he confided in her, that she felt needed. Cinda's experience with her absent father coupled with her mother's open disdain for men had severely damaged Cinda's ability to trust men. She felt fortunate to have found a man who she thought would never leave her.

When Cinda saw James holding back negative emotions, certain that she understood him, she was able to induce him into talking about his deep feelings. She noticed James pursing his lips together and lowering his face when in front of the king, and she encouraged him to express his feelings to her once they were alone. She loved the little boy she saw in James and felt safe with him. In bed at night, she dreamed about how they would conquer the world together.

James also believed he knew what to do in order to find everlasting happiness. Like many young men, he spent the first years of his marriage in pure contentment. He admired Cinda's assertiveness toward others because he saw strength in her that he wished he had.

The royal couple finally drift off to sleep, lost in happy memories of the past, but each is still deeply troubled by the unwelcome changes that have come their way and marred their happiness.

Questions:

Do you remember the way you acted and reacted towards your partner during the romantic phase of your marriage?

What ways did you treat him or her then that you are forgetting to do now?

5

The Ultimatum

$\mathcal{T}$he years pass, and two beautiful children join the family. After the romantic phase of the marriage fades away, the next phase—realization, sets in, for which they were both ill-prepared.

The couple spends less time talking and dreaming together. James spends more and more time away from the castle, attending to affairs of state and ultimately avoiding the problems at home, and Cinda's tenuous sense of security, already on shaky ground, begins to crumble as she starts to feel that James's other concerns are taking priority. In response, she begins to fall into patterns established by her mother and she unwittingly unleashes her anger and criticism, which James once thought a strength, onto her partner and her servants. Her treatment of the staff begins to bother James, but in fear, he does nothing and walks away, attempting to ignore the situation.

Only Morella, a childhood companion of Cinda's, appears to be free from her wrath. Cinda continues to confide in and trust Morella as she pushes James further and further away.

James no longer views Cinda as admirable. In fact, he feels so insecure with her that he wants to flee. In spite of his growing awareness, James holds his feelings deep within, still clinging to love-induced blindness. His refusal to address these frightening feelings institutes a pattern that when left unaddressed continues to worsen. He ignores Cinda's outbursts, thinking it better to say nothing than to risk losing what happiness they have left. Although he ponders the change in their relationship from strong and nurturing to its present state of turmoil and distrust, he does not look inside himself for answers; instead, he denies his feelings and perpetuates the unhealthy pattern. And so, the couple has reached their current desperate state. Both feel that they are approaching a critical point at which the relationship will either overcome the difficulties or break down altogether.

Satori watches. He knows from past experience that the child within each person never stops dreaming and never gives up belief in magic, and so it is for James and Cinda. Long past the honeymoon, two beautiful children, good intentions, and the material wealth and luxury of a palace cannot provide the couple with the skills they need for the give and take that must exist in any healthy marriage.

After several days of silence and many sleepless nights for both, James gathers his courage and approaches Cinda. "Cinda, we have to talk. We can't go on like this anymore."

Cinda pretends, as was her practice in childhood that nothing is wrong. She hesitantly replies, "What do you mean?"

James, stunned by her level of denial, stands speechless a moment, trying to compose a response. "You must know, my dear. How many times have you turned away from me when I have reached out for you?"

Cinda, not wanting to show her anxiety, lowers her voice and looks directly at James. "I have seen your face when you are angry, even though you try to hide it. It frightens me."

James shifts uncomfortably, fighting the urge to retreat into silence. He gathers his courage and boldly continues to press the issue. "After all of these years, Cinda, I sense your coldness and suspicions. Why can't you see that I love you?"

Cinda is unsettled by James's words and asks with mock incredulity, "What suspicions? What are you talking about?"

Taking a deep breath and squaring his shoulders, he continues. "Don't pretend that you can't remember all the times you have accused me of being unfaithful."

Her heart pounding, Cinda turns away from his gaze. "I don't know, James. I simply do not know."

Aghast, James feels his anger taking over. Cinda uses denial the way he has seen his father do. He goes on the offensive, attempting to defend himself against unspoken accusations. "I have showered you with gifts and given you everything you have asked me for. I have nothing to feel guilty about!"

Cinda's suspicions are aroused. She thinks, *He must be hiding something. Otherwise, why would he speak of guilt?* As she continues to pretend ignorance, James's negativity, passed down from his father, is brewing inside of him.

Cinda finally replies bitingly, "I find this whole conversation ridiculous. I have not accused you of anything. If you have a guilty conscience, that is your business."

Furious, James responds, "Cinda, I cannot go on like this anymore. Your accusations have got to stop. Are you so deluded that you believe that I would satisfy your whims only to cover up my affairs?"

Cinda, with feigned nonchalance, replies, as she heard her mother do so often, "Men do it all of the time."

James shoots right back, "Maybe men do—but not this man. I have integrity, my dear. I could have any woman in the kingdom at any time, but I've only ever wanted you."

Eyes welling with tears, Cinda struggles to hold in the doubts and fears that have plagued her for so long. Finally, unable to hold them any longer, she bursts out, "Why? You hardly compliment me anymore. You walk away from our conversations. Why do you avoid me? And did you ever stop to realize that I don't like you ordering me around like your father does your mother? Do you ever hear what I say to you? You want to talk, but you never listen."

James had been oblivious to this resentment under the surface of Cinda's apparent confidence up to this point. He buries the anger he feels inside when Cinda ignores his questions and quietly blames himself instead, a habit learned from childhood. Softly, he says, "I listen to you."

Cinda, still angry, replies, "No, you don't, James."

As James goes over their repeated conversations in his mind, unable to confront the larger issues facing them, he focuses on a lesser subject that has been a point of contention between them for a long time. "If this is about my old servant Charles, you are off base. It is you who does not listen to me. I told you that Charles is my business, not yours. Yet you continue to want to control what I do with him."

The argument shifts away from the deeper problems and onto a more superficial one. Cinda, on firmer ground, recollects herself and replies defensively, "I'm not trying to control you or your life. It's just that you obviously are not dealing with the situation. Charles is getting old. Maybe he needs to retire."

James's anger rises again and he snaps back, "There you go again, telling me what to do. Either we find help for our relationship, or this is the beginning of the end."

Shaking her head, Cinda walks to the window and looks out. "I refuse to discuss my affairs with anyone. They will tell the entire palace our business ... No, I will not do that."

"I will find someone discreet, someone who is sensitive and respectful of our situation," James pleads.

Cinda stubbornly reiterates, "I won't go."

James sinks slowly into a nearby chair. He sighs and says resignedly, "And I won't stay."

Cinda, still burdened with the feelings of abandonment and unworthiness from childhood, gathers all of her courage to ask, "If you do not love me, why did you choose me?"

James looks up at her. "How ..." he begins incredulously. Then deciding to steer the argument back to firmer ground, he starts again. "Our conversations about Charles have nothing to do with my love for you. I just don't want you to talk about Charles's faults with me. He has been like a father to me, and I will not put him out to pasture like an old horse! This is about my love and respect for Charles. It has nothing to do with you, or us."

Cinda turns to face James. Believing herself misunderstood, she feels James's attack unfair. "Why didn't you just tell me before how you felt instead of walking away?"

James pauses for a moment before finally responding, "I don't know. Maybe it's your tone of voice. Or maybe it's because I resent you trying to control me. I had too much control as a child, and I won't accept it as an adult."

Finally, Cinda's tears overwhelm her considerable self-control and she breaks down and cries inconsolably. James's attitude has brought painful memories of her mother to the surface.

In frustration, James stands up and begins to pace. He says accusingly, "This is why I cannot talk to you about my feelings! Whenever I do, you act as if I have stabbed you in the back! When you cry like this, I feel like a failure as your husband. I retreat and walk away. What else can I do?"

Cinda, still crying, does not respond. When James yells, she feels overpowered and helpless. She is unable to match his tirade. Meanwhile, James finally stalks out of the room in frustration, thinking, *This is how most of our conversations end. We continue to go around the same circle until Cinda breaks down and cries. How can I express my feelings to her when she won't listen? Why doesn't she understand that what I am saying is not about my love for her, but is about my love for Charles?*

Cinda sees the situation differently. When James walks away, she sees it as proof that he doesn't love her. It was what her mother used to do. She concludes that he must reserve his affections for those who have been around his whole life, like Charles. Her insecurity gets the better of her as she thinks, *I just know that Mother is right. Any day now, he will leave me just as my father left.*

Satori hears all. He can see that both parties mean well and wonders how so much confusion and anger arises. "The seeds of goodness are in all of us even while we are here for our lessons, for we come from a source of love."

Questions:
What happened to you as a child that damaged your ability to trust?

6

James Makes a Decision and a Friend Proves False

*C*inda keeps her unhappiness inside, not daring to tell anyone how she feels. She asks herself why she doesn't appreciate James anymore and feels guilty for thinking these thoughts. But as James becomes more and more distressed about his once so ideal marriage, he is becoming desperate for advice. His mother had taught him to reach out for help when necessary, while Cinda's mother made her feel ashamed for asking. She made Cinda feel small if she didn't know it all.

Early in his marriage, James's mother, Queen Elayna, had warned him that the transition might be difficult for Cinda and he would have to help her. "Cinda does not yet know what to do. Your lifestyle is still too new for her; in time, she will learn. For now, my son, you must be strong and teach her how to be a princess."

However, James is disappointed with the outcome of his attempts to follow this counsel. He consoles himself with thoughts like, *I have done my best to set an example, but it does no good.* However, he inwardly admits that he does not know how to teach Cinda to be a princess because he is not feeling confident in what he knows.

Not knowing what is happening within or where else to turn he enters the rebellious stage of marriage. He seeks out Cinda's closest friend, Morella, thinking she, as Cinda's confidante, can help him understand his wife. James is aghast when he hears what she has to offer. His suspicion of her motives is aroused, but he is desperate for answers.

Looking at James with sympathy, Morella shakes her head sadly and says, "Cinda has no understanding of men. She won't change. She will continue to criticize you, just as her mother criticized her father. At her core, she is a very negative person." Morella pauses and sighs dramatically before continuing. "You know I love Cinda, but … I feel it is my duty to be honest and warn you."

Morella's poisonous words shock James. The advice throws him into a frenzy. He feels he should dismiss Morella's comments out of loyalty to Cinda, but in spite of his good intentions, James weighs this warning as he remembers Cinda's complaints, telling James all that is wrong with him. James's anger and his fear of his father rise to the surface. He has always reacted in this way, usually with disastrous consequences.

Morella, feeling confident in her powers of persuasion, boldly encourages more doubt in James's mind by hinting that Cinda did not marry him for love. "If I were your princess, I would always be loyal to your dreams—as Cinda once was. But Cinda cannot continue to support you. She does not have the conviction of love to fall back upon."

From afar, Satori continues to watch, wait, and assess the relationship. He has seen in his work with other couples that the early voices of our mothers and fathers lodge in our minds. It is not long before our childhood selves, negative and insecure, fiercely step forward into our adult relationships. If these early childhood wounds are not addressed, they will fester and cause irreparable damage.

Lacking in awareness, Cinda and James's love cannot deepen and nourish them. Their struggle worsens. Although Cinda has married the handsome prince of her dreams, the child within her that does not feel loved begins to protest. Due to her early wounds, Cinda does not have the ability to fully trust anyone, even her husband, and she too struggles with asserting herself. How could she then begin to trust her husband, a man, whose treacherous nature her mother so often warned her about?

> It is difficult, if not impossible, for true love to flourish without each having a healthy understanding of why they are reacting as they do.

James, without much-needed self-confidence and fearing criticism, has a difficult time when Cinda expresses her feelings. Because he fears telling her his truth, he avoids confrontations by leaving on a business trip or an overnight visit to the king and queen. Cinda then feels more alone and unloved, as her fear of abandonment deepens.

It is difficult, if not impossible, for true love to flourish without each having a healthy understanding of why they are reacting as they do.

Cinda and James's troubled relationship gives them no comfort. When problems with the king and with the children arise, neither has the ability to hear the other. Cinda does not listen when she feels abused, and James walks away thinking that he is avoiding the problem. They are both exhibiting the negative behaviors they saw so often in their parents.

Satori sees a spark of hope, though, and believes all is not lost. During the moments when Cinda allows herself to move close to James, he willingly responds. Thus, the magic of love is still there. But when James avoids her, the frightened voice of Cinda's inner child appears, and she begins to criticize James mercilessly, not knowing what else to do and unaware that she is acting just like her mother. In response, James's inner child is as frightened as he was when his father yelled, so he escapes to a safe haven as he did when a child.

Innocently, both begin to walk in their parents' shoes as they recreate the lives they grew up knowing.

Thoughts like, *If I could not trust Father, how can I trust James?* are never far from Cinda's mind. Encouraged by her scheming friend, Morella, Cinda decides not to allow herself to be vulnerable towards any man—sadly, even her dear prince. Morella applauds Cinda's good reasoning as she patiently awaits her downfall.

When Cinda's criticisms increase in intensity, James begins to distance himself from his princess and openly begins to be as critical as his father was. Although James has the feeling that he is beginning to sound like his father and walk in his parents' footsteps, his ego won't let him fully admit this, and therefore, he is unable to find other answers or make other choices.

Morella's words are so unnerving to his sensitive soul that James wisely turns to his inner self and his deep belief in the higher power for assistance. He vows to persevere. "I promise to do all that I can to strengthen my marriage, no matter what it takes."

Questions:
How do you react to blame or criticism from your partner?

7

Trouble in the Kingdom

$\mathcal{A}$s is often the case in life, when trouble is brewing in one area, it seems to spread to others. James, seeking relief from his marital problems, throws himself into his duties as prince. He makes some startling discoveries and learns that all is not well in the reign of King John.

Massive flooding in the lowlands for the past three years has plagued the kingdom, which has devastated homes and destroyed crops. Prince James worries that there will be a shortage of food and they will be forced to import food from abroad to fill in the gaps in supply. This concerns the young prince greatly because he knows his father has always spent extravagantly so the coffers are becoming increasingly bare while the cost of goods, particularly those that have to be shipped in, is rising.

In spite of James's repeated attempts to warn his father, the king stubbornly refuses to face the facts and change his ways. The kingdom is beginning to reap the consequences of the king's negligence. Prince James feels as if he carries the weight of the kingdom on his shoulders. It is his family's responsibility to attend to the needs of the small nation, and they are failing.

James dreads telling Cinda of these problems for fear that she will not know how to face them, and her reactions will only make his life more difficult. So he holds these feelings in, as life at home deteriorates. His mind torments him each night as he goes to bed. His nights are spent thrashing and turning in his sleep.

This night, he tortures himself once more with thoughts of his father's upcoming trip abroad to purchase a dozen white stallions. He knows that he will be trusted to pay because he is a king, but James wonders where the funds will come from. James wakes, unrested and concerned as to how to approach his father with the reality of the situation. This encounter with King John will be more serious than the first, and James fears that his father will again not listen.

He leaves the castle, completely obsessed by thoughts of what to do and who to turn to for help, and doesn't even realize that he has not kissed Cinda goodbye, nor wished her a good day, as is his practice. Cinda, feeling abandoned, is devastated and spends most of the morning crying.

Questions:

How did you feel when you were ignored or not listened to when you were a child?

How do you think it affects how you react to your partner today?

8

The Dream

Still troubled about his latest argument with Cinda and facing the kingdom's impending financial ruin, Prince James tosses and turns in bed for a second night in a row. Each day seems to bring added stress and apprehension. James wonders, *Where has my happiness gone? What has happened to the magic of our love? Why does my bride turn away from me in the night when I do all in my power to make her happy? Why is my little beauty sad and depressed? What is wrong?*

James is painfully aware of the effect Cinda's words and actions have on him, but he remains oblivious to the way he wounds her by not talking and walking away when they argue.

James tries to decide which of his problems is worse: Cinda or his father. He rolls over once again. At this moment, he feels as if he does not have the knowledge to handle either of them successfully.

The very last thing James wants is to get involved with another woman. Keeping his vows is very important to him. But the prince is lonely and beset by the temptations of the flesh offered to him by the maidens of the kingdom, including Cinda's best friend, Morella. His attempts to seek solace in his favorite pastime, fencing, even cause problems with Cinda. She accuses him of caring more about his friends and his sport than her. James is beginning to feel like a prisoner.

Tossing again, James fidgets uncomfortably as he remembers how upset Cinda was that he left the castle without saying goodbye. He assuages his guilt by blaming Cinda. *It reminds me of when I was a child and Mother would try to stop me from going out. My father took my side, saying no son of his would be a weakling.* James is still unaware that his thoughts revolve only around how he is treated and not the way he treats Cinda or how his reaction to her may be causing some of the friction.

Restless and still unable to sleep, James rises at 3:15 a.m. Determined to use the time for a good purpose, he puts on his midnight-blue, satin-trimmed robe, a gift from Cinda, and reaches for his shabby, worn-out tan suede slippers, favorites since his teenage days. In the castle chapel, he decides to pray and meditate all night long until he finds needed peace.

While deep in meditation, James drifts off to sleep. Still in a deep sleep, James feels a stirring within that startles him. A voice from the distance moves closer and closer until the vision of a man with a long, flowing white beard appears. James cannot make out the face or features of this mysterious figure.

The man speaks with a peace, harmony, and gentleness that James has not known before. "My son, I have seen your problems and will help you find a way to solve them." James, deeply grateful, knows the voice is an answer to his prayers.

The man speaks with strength and dignity. "Over the centuries, I have watched the havoc created in relationships. When apprehension steps in, it causes a lack of respect and appreciation. My son, your princess has fears that prevent her from understanding you. You, too, my prince, have a past riddled with apprehension and fear. Your uneasiness prevents you from hearing your princess."

Before James can respond, the voice continues, "When you become conscious of your fears, the doubts from your childhood will not resurface. Then you will experience pleasure and delight in appreciating each other once again. Your task is to learn how to set boundaries for yourselves so that love, understanding, and the pleasure of romance may return."

> When you become conscious of your fears, the doubts from your childhood will not resurface. Then you will experience pleasure and delight in appreciating each other once again.

James is amazed to have his problems addressed in such a profound but simple way. "And what of the financial problems, Father's neglect, and the devastation from the floods and ruined harvests? How can I handle so many problems at one time? I am only one man. What should I do?"

The superior being answers, "I have been here with you from the beginning, my son, and have been waiting for your request for help. Your wish is being granted as we speak. Together, we can help you find the way to handle all of your problems with confidence. We will help Cinda understand why her fear of losing you causes her to want to know your every move. You can learn to give her your strength, dignity, and emotional support, the qualities which attracted her to you in the beginning."

"And the problems with Father? How will you help there?" A few moments pass as James thinks, *Aha. He has no answer for this one.*

The voice finally answers, "Cinda's fears cause her to make you put yourself in a self-made prison. She is so afraid of losing the happiness she once found, that she tries to bottle it. Cinda does not know that by bottling you up, she loses the essence of what she loves so dearly."

As the superior being replies, James is astounded by the truth in his words. He remembers when Cinda hung on to his every word, desiring nothing more than to help him feel content, but he still wonders about his father.

James quietly asks, "What has happened to me?"

"When you allow her to do this to you, you lose the respect and appreciation she once had for you. Your father, too, has fears of being seen as a failure. Rather than face his problems, he continues to hide in them as his father and grandfather before him did. But the time has come that he cannot hide anymore."

James begins to see how his problems are all connected, but wonders what he should do.

"Release your suspicions and fears, and take the reins that you were meant to have. Feel the strength of conviction and purpose that you have within you, and prepare to speak your beliefs. Have faith in your dreams, and your spirit will become your own again—to find what it desires and do what it was meant to do. Achieve your destiny."

> Feel the strength of conviction and purpose that you have within you, and prepare to speak your beliefs.

James begins to feel some freedom within, but he has doubts.

The voice reassures him. "James, you could not have known the signs that were there in the beginning or recognize the fears that cause Cinda to keep you all to herself. Your fear of expressing your feelings prevents you from taking action with Cinda and your father, as well. Is this not true?"

James breathes in deeply before hesitantly admitting, "Unfortunately, I fear that speaking my truth will cause the magic of our love to disappear."

"Why, my son? Isn't it worse to hold your feelings inside and, by so doing, lose the love that you feel for your princess and the strength you have within?"

As some of his confidence returns, James allows himself to think about what brought him to this place. He nods slowly. "You are right. I must move away from my early beginnings ... you see, I was taught to keep my feelings inside. I fear that I will cause even more problems by speaking. I watched Mother try to express her thoughts, and it only made her situation worse."

A brief silence follows, and then the sage asks thoughtfully, "What happened to your mother?"

Without hesitation, James replies, "Mother retreated, and the king won. He always won."

"What caused her to retreat, my son?"

Sadness overtakes James. He puts his head down and barely whispers, "Her fear brought her down—always her fear."

"Your mother was here to teach you what not to do, my son. Remember her actions and the results, and you can make a different choice."

A look of surprise replaces the despair in the young prince's face. "That's it! It seems so obvious now. It is the same fear that I saw in Mother that is now holding me back." He jumps up from his chair enthusiastically. "Thank you ... I have been desperate for some guidance."

The wise one is not yet finished with the lesson, however. "When you keep your thoughts inside, does the pain not worsen and become more intolerable?"

Suddenly overwhelmed with the familiar feeling of self-blame, James cannot speak. He hears the voice again. "My son, stop blaming yourself or others. It will do no good. See this as a valuable lesson instead."

Wrinkling his brow quite perplexed, James says, "I am trying to understand how to apply this lesson. I do realize how it has relieved my worries. I know I still have a lot of work to do, but I now see a clearing through the trees."

After a long silence in the room, the sage speaks again. "When we do not learn and take action, love does begin to disappear. Is this not true?"

James agrees. "Yes, sadly, I had not thought of it this way before. My hope is always that our life will gradually improve. But you are right; taking no action causes nothing to change and much to worsen. I suspect the same advice applies to father as well."

"Yes, my son, fear not. There is no coincidence in all that happens. It is necessary that you, as a leader of men, are learning this lesson. For soon, it will be your turn to pass this newly acquired knowledge on to your kingdom. If your father, the king, could have taught you differently, he would have, but he did not have the understanding. Your time is here; you must be the one to do what is best for you, your family, and your kingdom."

James is learning that by not heeding the signs, the imperceptible seeds of their magical beginning are fading away. He slowly and thoughtfully admits, "In truth, I do not have deep feelings for my princess any longer, but neither do I want to fail in my marriage. I fear her anger—just as I do my father's. I now realize it is I who am preventing our love from moving forward."

The vision smiles sympathetically. "The signs are not to be feared, my son, but rather to be appreciated. They prepare you for the challenge of keeping the magic of love in your life. You are one of the most influential men in your kingdom; you are meant to become involved in learning to communicate authentically—a tool that will help you achieve all that you desire. Do you understand why?"

Suddenly, a light flashes in James's mind as he sees his purpose very clearly for the first time. "I must become a king who will one day lead the way toward understanding and communicating—both in love and managing my kingdom. I know that only I can change myself. That is why I'm faced with conquering my problems with both my father and Cinda. They both provide the lessons I must master before I can be the king I plan to be. Without business or love growing in the right direction, where will I be?"

James interrupts his own thoughts, saying, "If I am correct, when I ignore the signs, I fail to take the needed step of speaking my thoughts, and then my courage dissipates. By speaking my thoughts, my fears disappear and are replaced by a growing determination and ability to achieve my desires."

> By speaking my thoughts, my fears disappear and are replaced by a growing determination and ability to achieve my desires.

The wise one nods in agreement. "Yes. For example, it is indeed easy to complain about your spouse or your father to a trusted friend since you have no fear of repercussions. But if you tell Cinda or your father your true feelings, the response may be anger, criticism, mockery, or rejection—precisely what arouses your fears."

Understanding dawns on James. "You're right. With the fears I carry from childhood, it is no wonder that I keep my feelings hidden from Cinda and Father—although in different ways. Wouldn't you?"

The vision replies, "My son, each of us chooses a different path. For many of us, it is easier to deny our feelings and blame another instead."

"Thank you for your help." James clenches his jaw in determination. "I will heed your wise advice by replacing fear with courage, and blame with communicating. I will become a king of all kings. I will show my people a new way to create good, no matter how difficult it becomes ... Yes, I now realize that we must step outside of ourselves and watch, and we will see the lessons our god provides."

The sage's face remains impassive, but inside he thinks, *He shall become a king unlike any other.*

James now understands that choosing blame and fear is exactly what Cinda and the king do and what he has done as well. By not expressing himself fairly, he is creating his own chaos and unhappiness. Resolutely, James declares, "I am choosing to make the choice to be different."

The vision quickly affirms his choice. "Right, James. No matter what others do, you must have the courage to move forward."

James begins to stir in his sleep, feeling better than he has in the past several months. He says aloud, "I must help myself first, and not be afraid that by broaching the subject of my feelings, I will lose the magic of love; if I do, then it must have not been there in the first place."

The image of the sage is beginning to grow fainter. His voice is quieter as he congratulates the prince on his progress and gives him one last bit of advice. "Good, my son. A king must have wisdom and courage and not give in to fear. By expressing your feelings, in spite of difficulty, you are watering the seeds of strength. And, in time, you will see the seeds sprout, allowing love's enchantment to return once again. You will have the courage to create the kingdom of your dreams. Your kind of 'right over might' shall be different from kings past—and why not? These are different times."

Lost in contemplation, James suddenly realizes he is missing an important bit of information. "But wait, I don't know who you are ..." Before the sage can respond, the dream ends, and James can no longer see the vision.

Questions:

What were you taught about expressing yourself as a child?

Did you have to hide your true feelings in order to get your needs met?

9

Satori's Path

Each day for the past several years, Satori has watched and waited and contemplated the delicate balance of the relationship between Cinda and James. His goal is not only to help the prince and princess with their struggling relationship, but also to teach humans this wisdom and how to pass it on to others. The sage knows that he is only one man; although he is powerful and wise, his reach is limited.

As Satori returns from a long trek towards the summit of another high peak, he appreciates the beauty of this breathtakingly glorious day. After his exhilarating climb, Satori begins a deep and rejuvenating meditation. He looks forward to a good night's sleep.

In the middle of the night, while in a dreamlike state, Satori is blessed with a clear and vivid epiphany. There before his eyes appears a second vision of Prince James seeking the answers to his marital problems. This time, Satori sees himself in his purple satin robe seated before

Cinda and James, as he helps them to successfully begin communicating and, slowly but surely, to leave their anger behind.

Satori is elated. His vision has shown him that with one good hour, the couple can begin to once again feel the essence of each other. He resolves to put the vision to the test. He remembers all the couples painstakingly climbing this great mountain to seek his wisdom in the past. Shaking his head, he admonishes himself; *I must not feel badly for my failures of the past. All of that was only in preparation for what is to come.*

Still deep in thought, with a broad, contented smile, Satori gives thanks for being allowed to be part of opening the pathways of communication for humankind, for this tool will be vital in replacing swords, armor, and kill-

> Giving begets giving. When one gives from the heart, without asking anything in return, one's own desires are fulfilled in the process.

ing. His pupil is a leader of men. Satori thanks the gods for allowing him to be the catalyst for James, soon to be king and leader of men. With Princess Cinda at his side, James could be the one to help people develop the essential skills of communication.

Satori feels a deep gratitude, for James's plea is in turn helping him. He muses, "Giving begets giving. When one gives from the heart, without asking anything in return, one's own desires are fulfilled in the process."

The sage knows it will take time and perseverance for James and Cinda to learn new patterns of behavior.

Although his vision portends a bright future, he knows he must have a great deal of patience and be certain of the exact moment to manifest himself in person to James. His path will be to sow the seeds of knowledge that will grow and spread from James and Cinda to the entire populace.

With a great sigh of relief, feeling replenished by his new vision, Satori knows he has chosen most worthy subjects. As the young prince grows stronger by studying the wise words of his mentor, Cinda, too, will be influenced. Satori has assessed her character and decided she is equally strong in spirit and a suitable partner for James.

Satori does not allow himself to doubt that he will succeed. He is determined to persevere in his quest.

Questions:
What are your beliefs about sharing wisdom with others?

10

Providence Takes Its Course

*J*ames awakens at 6:00 a.m. as usual. His faithful manservant, Charles, greets him and serves him a hearty breakfast. Charles has known James from early childhood and loves him dearly. He is thrilled and relieved to see James's change of mood.

Charles would admire the princess if James were happy, but seeing the unhappiness in James, who is like a son to him, he finds that he is not an admirer of Cinda's. Charles has confidence that James's sense of integrity and discipline are integral parts of who he is and will guide him until he has succeeded. However, Charles is wise enough to understand that there are two people at work in every relationship.

As James peers out his bedroom window, he fixes his eyes upon the lush beauty of the trees and flowers surrounding the majestic grounds of the castle. With a renewed sense of optimism, James says to Charles, "It is as beautiful outside this morning as my heart is cheerful."

Bursting with enthusiasm, James prepares for his daily routine of walking through his beloved woods, a place of refuge and happy memories. He takes out his favorite boots and an old pair of corduroy trousers.

In high spirits and with newly found energy, James is unconsciously convinced that he is being guided to meet his destiny: the wise man from his amazing dream.

Charles intuitively understands what James is feeling. "My royal highness, my wishes are with you. Is there anything I can do?"

Touched by Charles's words, James turns his head as he finishes dressing. "Thank you, Charles."

Excited and refreshed, James proceeds on his way. His two brown and black spotted hunting dogs bark in anticipation of a walk, but today, Prince James wants to be alone. He pats them with affection but leaves them running in their enclosed yard.

As James walks through the woods and looks up at the clouds, he believes his god knows what he is feeling, and he bows his head in prayer. "Thank you, dear Lord, for sending me the vision last night. I trust this is the day you will lead me to meet this wise man. I cannot proceed without you." Instantly, as if in response, the sun bursts through the clouds and casts a bright light over the land.

On his way to the pond, the prince comes upon the three majestic trees that he used to climb as a child. Once again, he feels the spirit of this very sacred place calling to him. He had come here as a child when in need of strength and help.

In his mountain retreat, Satori feels the vibrations of James's call and prepares for his journey. He will be there in a moment, having mastered the art of transcending laws of space and time. Satori calls his much treasured companion, his dog Woodrow.

Woodrow, affectionately known as Woody, was deposited on Satori's doorstep as a tiny puppy. Since that day, he has been Satori's constant and faithful companion. Woodrow is nearly as famous as Satori. Like many of his species, Woodrow is intuitive to the emotions and needs of the humans with whom he shares his world.

He is small enough to fit into a lap. His soft, flowing blond fur, floppy ears, and large, deep, dark brown eyes have comforted many over the centuries. The enchanted dog peers directly into a person's eyes, the windows of the soul, and empathically communicates his feelings. He offers those working with Satori emotional support and that rarely felt and much-needed gift—unconditional love.

Satori looks to Woodrow for cues to the deepest feelings inside men while he teaches. The sage recognizes the remarkable healing powers of the animal world, and its benefits to lonely human souls without the ability to develop intimacy with their closest relationships.

Without hesitation, Satori begins his descent down the mountain, knowing exactly where to find the magic portal to James's realm. In moments, he is waiting with Woodrow deep in the woods of Lavonia.

Questions:
What are your beliefs in a higher power?

11

The First Meeting

$\mathcal{S}$atori and Woodrow are sitting in James's childhood sanctuary deep in the woods just meters from where James kneels absorbed in prayer. Woodrow begins gleefully jumping up and down, tugging at Satori's shabby shirtsleeves and jolting him from the relaxed meditative state that follows his passage through the magical portal.

Satori smiles in satisfaction; he knows full well that he can always rely on his beloved companion. He feels the vibrations of James pleading for him to come forth.

Patting Woodrow's silky head, Satori prepares to face his destiny.

Although eager to meet the prince, Satori takes out an old and battered book, one of his most sacred, and reads softly aloud, "A prince must have wisdom to attract to himself people of ability who are expert in directing affairs of the world. If he is consumed with affairs of the heart, he will not be able to help his people or to be conversant in the affairs of his kingdom.

"He who cultivates the inferior parts of his nature is an inferior man. He who cultivates the superior parts of his nature is a superior man. If owing to weakness of spirit, a man cannot support himself, a feeling of uneasiness comes over him. Thus he must turn from his accustomed path and beg counsel and help from a man who is spiritually his superior, but undistinguished."[1]

Humbly, Satori quietly wonders if his skills are a match for the monumental problems facing this future monarch.

It seems like hours to James, who is still in prayer and longing for answers. Then, as if in the midst of yet another dream, James hears the three trees begin to rustle. Speechless, with eyes wide open, he watches as an ethereal entity approaches. As the figure comes closer, James perceives a soft, cloudlike light emanating from and surrounding the man's entire body. James feels a purity and serenity he has never felt before. He can hardly contain his excitement, as he believes divine providence is interceding.

The barking of a dog disturbs his vision. Looking around, he at first sees nothing, but as he turns toward the sound, James feels a tugging at his heels. Deeply annoyed at the interruption, he believes his pants are caught on a tree stump. "This is all I need! What else will go wrong today?"

Then, as if out of nowhere, James hears a soothing voice calling, "Woodrow, where are you leading me?" Quickly, James looks up, and before him stands a powerful figure of a man with a long, flowing white beard and sparkling eyes as blue as the tropical ocean.

---

[1] I'Ching

As their gazes meet, recognition flashes in James's mind. "You are the vision I saw in last night's dream! What a miracle!"

Eager to acquaint himself with such a powerful being, James at last remembers to ask, "Who are you?"

"It is I, Satori, my son. I am here to guide you to uncover the answers to your prayers and to help you learn that the true value of love begins with knowing thyself from within."

"Satori? I think I have heard tales of you, but I thought you were only a nice myth."

The sage chuckled. "Do I look like a myth?"

Reddening slightly, James forges on. "I am over-whelmed. I want to believe you, since you are here and you are indeed the sage who appeared to me in my dream last night."

Satori indicates to James that he should follow. The prince and the sage walk together deeper into the woods and continue to talk. James gratefully asks, "How can I repay you, Satori, for your help?"

Satori smiles at the eager young prince. "I am grateful to be chosen to help you, a prince who will be helping many men in need. This is my destiny, as well as yours."

James takes comfort in Satori's words. "It is one of my greatest desires to be able to help the people of my kingdom."

Satori's next words come as a bit of a surprise to James. "You, James, are beloved by your entire kingdom. Sadly, neither your wife nor you truly understand who you really are. Cinda does not trust you as yet, nor does she truly understand the sensitivity of your nature. My son, you too will need to learn to trust yourself. When Cinda learns to trust herself, she will learn to trust you."

James studies the older man carefully. *How can this man know so much—even my wife's name? Perhaps he really is the Satori of legend.* James has difficulty fully assimilating all he is hearing. He senses he is on the threshold of receiving relief from his present struggles, and so he is determined to continue. "Thank you for all of your encouragement. In truth, Satori, I feel like a royal failure at this moment—no pun intended. Can you help Cinda and me with the problems that now plague our relationship?"

"Yes, my son." The sage pauses, looks James in the eyes, and continues, "But it will require diligence on your part and a commitment to change. Are you ready and willing to take on this task?"

"More than ready," James replies without hesitation.

Satori laughs and smiles with a sigh of relief. "I knew you would be, my son. That is why I am here. I have been long awaiting your call for help. I left my homeland as soon as I heard you."

James's eyes widen in disbelief. "You heard me?"

"Indeed, I was with you in your dream."

"But how?"

Satori decides it is time to reveal more of his own story to James. "My son, I have been with you ever since the day of your birth. I was asked to look after you—as you are indeed a special being, brought on this earth to be a leader of men who one day will enthusiastically follow you."

James's body relaxes for the first time in months as he breathes deeply and looks on with hope. "Thank you,

Satori. To be honest, I have been expecting you, or someone. I knew my god would not let me down. Can we begin
immediately?"

"Certainly, my son. I have waited for this day for
years."

Jumping right in, James says, "Given the sad state of
my marriage, I am at a loss as to how to deal with Princess
Cinda. I must tell you this prevents me from being able to
focus on attending to the affairs of state."

Satori looks at James knowingly, full of love and compassion. "I plan to help you battle the storm and will be at
your side to help you develop to your fullest potential. It is
what the gods wish for a future king, a ruler of all men."

James sighs wearily and looks down at the ground.
"It will be a battle because the storm has come with two
fronts—business and love. Although I want to tackle the
problems in my relationship with Cinda, if I do not deal
with Father and the business of our impending economic
collapse, there may not be a kingdom left."

The sage remains silent, listening intently. James continues, "I realize that I must get my house in order before I
can become a leader of men. But it seems that I do not know
the ways of love or business or how to help my wife to be
happy and keep our kingdom afloat at the same time."

Woodrow jumps on James's lap and starts to lick his
hands, arms, and then his face.

In spite of himself, James laughs. "With such a partner, I see that you mean business. I already have faith in
you and now in your dog. How in the world does he know
how much I need his affection?"

"Woody understands the human heart. The gods have blessed me with this delightful assistant, and I am forever grateful."

Questions:

Do you intend to find a mentor whom you can trust for guidance and wisdom?

12

James Confronts His Fears

*S*atori advises James that the imminent financial collapse of the kingdom must be handled first. He knows James will find the strength and confidence he needs in his personal relationship if he can first apply them to this more external relationship.

James immediately explains his concerns to his newfound confidant. "I cannot stand by and watch Father ignore the needs of the economy anymore. It is infuriating to see Father continue the same spending habits he learned from my grandfather and great-grandfather. Times have changed, and our kingdom cannot sustain the king's denial of reality another day."

Before the wise man can respond, James abruptly adds, "Satori, if only I could tell you what I fear the most."

Satori gestures with his hand for James to continue. "Please speak candidly so that you can go right to what is upsetting you so."

The relief James feels to be able to express his fears to an actual human rather than a dream entity is evident. "I fear that when I finally take the reins of the kingdom, there will be no kingdom left. We could lose everything because of Father's irresponsibility. He is not aware of anyone but himself."

Satori smiles, to James's surprise. "Is this the time to be laughing at me, Satori? Do I not have enough problems to contend with?" he asks a bit testily.

The wise man raises his hands in surrender. "I am not laughing at you, my son; it just amazes me how well the universe gets its message across. It is indeed time for change."

Still confused, James says, "But I don't understand what you are implying."

"By having two of the most important aspects of your life staring you in the face at the same time, you are receiving a message from the universe that cannot be ignored. You must take action now," the sage patiently explains.

Realizing that Satori understands all that he is facing, James calms himself. "I see what you are saying. Cinda disregards my feelings, and Father disregards my advice. Both of them disrespect me. My marriage and my kingdom are in disarray. I'm afraid that my arguments with Cinda are harming our children. I'm glad the universe is forcing me to look directly at what is happening."

Gathering his courage, James goes on. "You say I must take action, Satori, and I know that you are right. But what should I do? All of my worries seem to be hitting me at the same moment. I have just spent another morning arguing with Cinda. I know that she is not aware that she is acting like her mother, but it still makes me angry.

"Now, in addition, I have to face the possibility of financial collapse at the hands of the king. I believe Father has untrustworthy people surrounding him—perhaps they are hoping to see our kingdom bankrupt so they can take over the reins. They may even be stealing from the royal treasury. Unfortunately, I have no supporters in court and am not in a position to confront them."

Satori's steps slow and he turns to face James. "My son, any good soldier will tell you not to tackle two fronts at one time, the odds are overwhelming. Do you agree?"

James nods.

"Then the answer is before you."

James ponders what Satori has said and reaches his own conclusion. His confidence returns and he knows what he must do. "I must stop walking on eggshells. I definitely have to speak to the king, without fear."

Satori smiles.

James continues, "I will get all of my facts and information in order so that there is no way Father can deny what is happening."

"You are quite right, my son. I suggest that you take one step at a time. When one is done well, you will be ready to move on to the next. That way, you are handling problems as they arise and will not be overwhelmed so much so that you cannot take action."

James thanks his mentor and makes his way back to the castle, muttering to himself, "The king, my marriage, the children … I will take one step at a time. After all, I am only a man. I thank you, God, for sending me help from above. I know I cannot handle all of this myself."

Satori walks away with a new spring in his step. He is well pleased that James is taking action.

~~~~~~

Questions:
What are some fears that you have not expressed?

~~~~~~

13

James Faces His Father

*A*s the prince's meeting with King John approaches, he can feel himself gaining confidence. Assured of the rightness of his cause and with the advice and encouragement of the wise sage, James proceeds with his plan without hesitation. In the past, when James sought to persuade his father, he had not come prepared with the necessary evidence.

Today is different. James has researched every detail of the economy. He knows the costs of the floods and ruined crops and the status of funds in the treasury. He will tell the king precisely where expenses can be cut and how much will be needed to put the kingdom on its feet and the path to recovery. He also has dossiers on every man in the court, if needed.

As James enters the royal chambers, he stands tall, filled with confidence. He knows he is ready to take this important step. Sure of his beliefs, James no longer feels the fear, anger, and hatred he has felt toward his father all of his life. A new feeling arises in the young prince: pity.

Under his breath, he says, "Thank you, Father, for teaching me what not to do. I now have the confidence to do what I must and not hide behind blame or misfortune. There is no turning back. I am doing what I must."

The king senses James's new level of confidence and is both surprised and pleased by it. He says to himself, "This is the son I have always wanted. I don't know what has brought on this change, but I feel proud of the assurance and confidence I sense in him."

At first, when James presents his father with the reality of the financial crisis facing the kingdom, the king laughs as usual and does not take him seriously. Attempting to cover his own shame at the mess he created for the kingdom, he labels James an alarmist. James perseveres as his father speaks of his concern as if it were merely a trifle and James an unrealistic dreamer. He encourages himself. *If I do not look at the problems facing us, nothing will change.*

After taking a moment to relax, and breathing deeply three times as he observed the sage doing, James realizes that the king's insulting remarks are defensive moves to protect him from assuming responsibility for his mistakes. James continues speaking, ignoring his father's insults. In the past, he would have gotten upset and walked away as he had seen his mother do and as he did with Cinda. Today, James is a new man. He shows the king irrefutable proof of the dishonesty of some of the men in his court.

He concludes, "Father, this information can no longer be ignored. I am calling an emergency meeting of your court and presenting the facts as they stand." He beckons a courtier and conveys his order to convene the court.

In minutes, the throne room is filled with men in various states of dishevelment and curiosity.

At the meeting, the king watches as some men make hasty attempts to smooth over the facts, while others do not even attempt to justify their behavior. They make no suggestions for correcting the shortfall, but instead arrogantly laugh and declare James a fool who does not know what he is talking about.

Denial will no longer work; the king's eyes are open now. He sees that his court will quickly change sides in order to keep their positions—even if it means being disloyal to him. James is vindicated, as it becomes clear that they have been waiting for the day when they can seize power from the king.

James is aware that his newly developed resolve is helping him. Standing up to his father with facts in hand, James has won. The respect of his father, which James has yearned for all of his life, is finally his.

Quietly, the king dismisses the court, announcing that he will take the time to study the documents. The men leave, still certain that they have won.

But that evening, the king has a difficult time sleeping and wakes up in a sweat. The truth had been thrust before him in court that day. He does not like what he saw. The courtiers behaved towards him as he had towards his son.

The next day, James is astonished when his father tells him, "My son, it is time for me to turn over the reins of power to you. You have proven yourself beyond a shadow of a doubt. We will plan a ball in honor of your coronation after your next birthday."

James holds out his hands to grasp his father's arms. "Thank you for your faith in me. I will not let you—or our people—down," he promises.

Questions:
What would give you the courage to express concern to the parent you have had the hardest time dealing with?

14

James Learns About Happiness

$\mathscr{S}$atori is jubilant over James's success with the king, but he knows it is only the beginning. Satori ponders how he can best help James to see the importance of developing self-knowledge even though he still suffers from the blindness of love.

Soon, James arrives and echoes his thoughts. "Satori, now that I have dealt successfully with Father, I want to put my marriage in order. My heart is heavy. Can we talk about that today?"

"Certainly, my son. I am here for you. Please do not hesitate to speak freely and openly," Satori encourages him.

"For the past seven years, I have diligently tried to provide the perfect life for my princess. I have tried to relieve her of stress and worry, but to no avail. It seems her unhappiness from childhood returns to her. But, worst of all, she doesn't seem to appreciate the luxurious lifestyle we are fortunate enough to have. No matter what I do, she is not affectionate or even polite."

"My son, why do you think it is your work alone to make your princess happy?"

A look of confusion crosses James's face. "That is my job as her husband. Isn't it?"

Satori shakes his head and gently corrects him. "No matter how much you love Cinda, she must discover for herself what she needs for true contentment."

James replies sarcastically, "Satori, Cinda thinks of what she wants every day. She always seems to have a new request, but no matter what she buys, it doesn't seem to satisfy her."

Satori sighs. "Oh, if only material advantages could feed our souls. Property, possessions, and wealth cannot meet our longing for happiness. We must go within to find what is missing in our lives."

> We must go within to find what is missing in our lives.

James had not thought of this. He asks the sage how one can feed one's own soul.

Satori explains, "Each one of us is truly responsible for our own happiness. While it is important to nurture one another, we must first know how to nourish our own source of being."

Lost in his sadness and self-pity, James does not grasp the wisdom behind the words. "Satori, what am I supposed to do when my wife treats me so badly?"

"James, you, too, must learn how to nurture your own soul. That means, first and foremost, you must respect yourself—a daunting task for all mankind. How can you love another when you have not learned how to love and respect yourself?"

James nods slowly, understanding beginning to come to him. He has been so focused on trying to mitigate Cinda's unhappiness, he has not thought of his own.

Satori continues, "All of the material possessions you have given her cannot fulfill her innermost needs."

"I know you're right. She has what most people dream about, but still each day, she finds something to complain about. Nothing will satisfy her. I buy her imported blue silk; she must have red, and later green. Even then, she is still not pleased. She has the world at her feet, but she is not content. How can I help her to understand that life is not perfect, even when I do all in my power to satisfy her latest whim?"

Woodrow, sensing James's pain, jumps up and curls up in his lap. James pats Woodrow and relaxes.

"Now I'm concerned that when she becomes queen, she will be insatiable and have no concern for the suffering of the people. The welfare of my people is very important to me." James pauses a moment. "I must be totally truthful with you, Satori. I no longer have any desire to help Cinda get what she wants. I feel like she is a bottomless pit, with no sense of appreciation for all of her good fortune," James continues bitterly.

Satori notices the anger and resentment James is feeling in not wanting to continue to satisfy his princess. "James, did you also try and fail to make your mother happy when you were a child?"

James at first denies any such feeling, but as he considers his childhood, he finally sees the truth in that statement.

"Ah, I see, my son. Now you erroneously think you must do the same for your princess. Am I correct?"

James accepts Satori's analysis, but still frustrated, he is intent on telling the wise man of the extent of his wife's mistreatment of him. "She tells me I do not love her anymore because I am turning a deaf ear to her newest reasons for being unhappy and disappointed each day."

Feeling as if he is not getting anywhere with James, Satori tries a new approach. "But, James, isn't it your job to make your princess happy? After all, you are her husband."

James squirms, his face crimson in color. He feels Woodrow curling up closer as he accuses himself. *Satori is right. What is wrong with me that I am powerless to make Cinda happy?*

James hears Satori chuckle and looks up and sees his blue eyes twinkling.

James recoils, feeling as if he is in the middle of a horrid nightmare. Satori continues, "You are right, James. You are a royal failure."

James, in shock, clenches his fists and glares back at the sage with the first hint of defiance. "I will not take this kind of abuse. I feel like I'm with Cinda."

Satori, having made his point, tells James what he knows to be true. "You see, my son, no one can make another happy. Wisdom cannot be communicated. One must delve into one's deepest feelings and learn from within oneself that which creates happiness. I have been egging you on, hoping you will see the absurdity of attempting such a task—to create happiness for your princess. It is her job, not yours. While you, as her husband, can provide a good life, Cinda alone must seek the true purpose for her own life. For it is purpose and giving to others that provide fulfillment. When one is focused on oneself only, happiness is elusive. My son, if you are trying to make your wife happy to the exclusion of your own contentment, you cannot succeed. For only resentment can come to you without sincere appreciation from your princess. And, as a result, you will only see your princess through angry and resentful eyes."

His good humor restored, James nods eagerly. "That is exactly what is happening. I am resentful of her lack of appreciation. My anger doesn't have an outlet so it festers, until I feel disgust towards the woman I once loved so dearly. In truth, I am no longer able to tolerate Cinda's closed world and trivial daily disappointments that are always about her and no one else. Nothing is ever good enough."

Satori shifts in his seat. "Do you now see that it is Cinda's job to find her contentment, and no matter how hard you try, you cannot do it for her? It only leads to you viewing Cinda in a light of negativity, making you ignore her positive traits."

James sighs deeply. "You mean I am not to blame? I have not failed in providing for Cinda as her husband? I understand now, Satori."

As Satori notices Woodrow leaving James's lap, he knows the prince is feeling better.

"James, the more you try, the worse it gets. Is that not so?"

"Exactly! I have run out of ways to calm and soothe her. When I see her bitter at the children, I cannot tolerate it. They don't deserve such treatment, even though I allow it for myself."

"Most children mirror their parents' behavior. Now, James, can you see that the children may also feel blame for Cinda's unhappiness, just as you do?"

"I hadn't thought of that. I can't allow this to happen to the children. They are innocent. Now can you see why I do not feel capable as a ruler of men when my own house is in such a state?"

"My son, once you realize your mistakes, you can correct them. What is important is your willingness to learn and to take action. It is not the problems that beset us but our desire to correct them that make a difference in our lives."

> Once you realize your mistakes, you can correct them.

"Thank you, Satori. I will sleep on your wisdom and return tomorrow, midday, if that is okay with you?"

"Yes, my son. I, too, have a mentor, as there are always new lessons for me to learn in this lifetime."

Satori smiles. He can see that James is becoming aware that he cannot create happiness for another, a most important concept. In good spirits, Satori says, "James, I venture to say that today is a very important day in your life."

James doesn't understand. "Please, Satori, no more puzzles. Just tell me what you mean."

"I think, my son, that you have learned man's greatest truth. You are not responsible for another's happiness. When you do the work for the other that they must do in life, they do not learn and the burden pulls you down."

"Yes," James agrees, "I understand that no one can escape the consequences of their actions. But is it really true that I am becoming unhappier the more I try to contend with Cinda's despondency?"

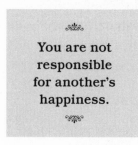

You are not responsible for another's happiness.

"My son, the reason you are so unhappy is that the harder you try, the less you feel you have succeeded. And, the more Cinda believes she can push you around, the less respect she feels for you. As a result, you have not love, respect, or appreciation."

"I can see the image of my parents' marriage in my life. Why have I recreated their marriage when mine started out so wonderfully?"

Satori looks at James with sympathy and understanding. "We each unknowingly walk in our parents' footsteps. It is the way of men. We have taken in our parents' traits, good and bad, since childhood. Contemplate this, and answers will come."

James sighs in relief. "I'm not to blame for being like my parents."

"No, my son. When you change the way you react to Cinda, you will no longer be forced to walk in your parents' shoes or to recreate their marriage. As of now, you are not conscious of the effect your reactions have on Cinda. Awareness is the first step towards personal and marital happiness. For without awareness, what are we? Unknowingly, each of us receives exactly what we give."

James studies his surroundings with a new sense of hope and purpose. "Now I see that today calls for a great celebration! I am learning life's most important truths."

Satori laughs a hearty laugh that fills the atmosphere with cheer. Mysteriously, he produces a bottle of premium claret and two goblets. He offers one to James, along with a toast: "And as Hamlet said, 'This above all: to thine own self, be true.'"

James toasts Satori. "To loving myself, a first step."

After a hearty toast, Satori and James part happily, each looking forward to their next time together.

Questions:
What incident in your childhood taught you that you could not provide happiness for another?

15

James Faces the Difficulty of Changing

*O*n this day, the third meeting, James is early. He paces anxiously back and forth, awaiting Satori's arrival. James's spirit seems much lower and somewhat depressed. His hair is askew. His chin is covered with stubble, and his clothes are somewhat wrinkled, unlike the enthusiastic man Satori had parted from yesterday.

Not wanting to waste a second of time, James immediately begins as soon as Satori arrives. "I am trying to follow your advice and have patience with Cinda. I realize that I must not run away from our problems. As I step aside and observe Cinda's outbursts, I am feeling less responsible for her feelings. But it seems my change is creating havoc within her. The less responsible I feel, the angrier Cinda becomes. What I am doing is not working."

The wise man peers into James's saddened eyes. "My son, what you are doing is likely right. It is part of the human condition. When you change the way you react towards the other, they do even more of what they are doing. Oftentimes, this is very confusing. But when what they are doing no longer works, they change the way they react to you.

"When Cinda recognizes that you are changing, and that her old ways of behaving no longer work, it is only then that the light will dawn and a new reality will begin to set in. She either will have to change the way she reacts towards you, or she, not you, will feel pain in your relationship. To date, you are the one who speaks of suffering, not Cinda. Is that an accurate assessment, James?"

"Exactly, but I hadn't thought of it that way."

"Well, there you have it, my son." Satori places his hand on the young man's shoulder. "The good news is that changes are coming. The bad news is that relationships get worse before they improve. Do not worry. I will be here to help Cinda when she is present and asking for help."

> When you change the way you react towards the other, they do even more of what they are doing. Oftentimes, this is very confusing.

After a quiet moment, James asks, "Why does such sadness have to come to those in love?"

"A good question. You see, many times, one, because of love, will do everything to make the other happy. This is not unusual. But when happiness does not come, the very same person feels responsible for the other's discontent. That person is usually the party that desires change. The other, no matter how unhappy, continues to place blame rather than take responsibility for the unhappiness."

James's eyes are intently fixed upon Satori as he puts the sage's words to memory.

"My son," he continues, "by changing the way you react to Cinda, you will be moving out of your usual pattern and progressing towards developing your own awareness, inner strength, and power. It is easier said than done, but I will guide you."

As James listens, he begins to stand taller with his shoulders squared, pride returning to his features.

Satori acknowledges the change. "I see a difference in your demeanor. What is happening within you?"

"I realize my eagerness caused me to behave quite differently last night," James replies.

"Yes, go on."

"It was quite a change for me, Satori. Last night, I responded without running into the next room or raising my voice, as I usually do. Instead, I stood my ground and said, 'Cinda, I am going to spend a few hours fencing with the boys.' As often happens, Cinda was not happy and eventually accused me of not loving her. Before showing my anger, I calmed myself and then said, 'Cinda, what I am proposing is about me, not you, and has nothing to do with love. I do love you, but I also want to spend some time with my friends. I plan to keep my word and return in a few hours.'

"Sad but true, my candid words did not help. As I was about to leave, Cinda ran after me, once again calling me the worst of names. I don't know if the children overheard us, but it was very bad. I never want to face this again. Now can you understand the reason why I rarely, if ever, tell Cinda my true feelings? The price is too steep to pay."

In a serious tone, Satori replies, "My son, did you stop to think of the fear that must be driving Cinda to react this way? Did you tell her that you would like to hear her feelings as soon as you return?"

"I was so upset that I didn't think it was about her. I was angry with her for making me feel controlled. But I also know that there is nothing wrong with playing sports with friends."

"My son, maybe Cinda's outburst was not about you, but about her."

"I see what you are saying, but should I have cancelled my plans like I did so many times before?"

"When you cancelled your plans before, how did you behave afterwards?"

"I would be so angry that I would not speak to her all evening."

"Then what did you accomplish by doing exactly what Cinda wanted? I suspect that her fears are so great that she is not even aware of what she needs."

"You are quite correct. I see now that what happens may not always be about me. Instead of blaming myself first, I must try to consider what is driving Cinda's behavior instead."

"Yes, my son, I suggest that next time this happens, you show understanding by telling Cinda that while you cannot cancel your plans once again, you do plan to talk about her feelings until you understand what is driving them when you return. You see, somewhere in your relationship, I know that you have unwittingly given her permission to act in this way towards you. She has responded in this way many times before, has she not?"

James nods.

"She continues to behave so because, in her mind, her behavior works. If it did not, she would not repeat it."

James stares at the ground deep in thought. "You're right. I have allowed Cinda to call me names and yell as loud as she can, which just causes me to feel more and more degraded. I have also allowed an incredible amount of anger to build inside of me."

"When have you expressed these feelings to Cinda?" Satori asks.

"Never. I just respond by leaving home and not coming back—sometimes for several hours, or even days."

"Yes, but when do you discuss what happened?"

"I already told you, never!" James snaps back. "Sometimes, it takes my whole being just to return. I often feel like I'm walking on eggshells, afraid of her responses."

> You have just taken a very brave first step.

Satori pauses, calming himself first and allowing time for James to assess what he is saying. Then in a purposefully calm and certain voice, he says, "That is in the past, my son. You have just taken a very brave first step. With continued practice, I promise, life will change for the better, and you will learn to accept and understand your feelings without internal shame. Avoiding communication only keeps the problems alive, but it is equally as important to set boundaries for yourself. You had quite a difficult time last night, but it was your first step towards speaking up for yourself and leaving fear behind."

Comforted and feeling calmer, James thanks his mentor for his advice and promises to act upon it. "I must admit, I do feel empowered, although I didn't feel that way last night."

"We will talk again tomorrow. I applaud you for standing up for your own beliefs. You deserve to feel proud of yourself."

Before James leaves, Satori adds, "Life is a continual work in progress. Is it not?"

Laughing and agreeing, James finally brings up a concern that has been troubling him. "Satori, I have been wondering how I can accomplish my goals with Cinda when she is not a part of our conversations. I'm afraid we are moving farther apart, and the gap is widening, rather than closing."

"Yes, my son. You are quite right. Let us consider bringing Cinda in here with both of us—when the time is right. I am glad you have broached this matter for discussion. I have been thinking for some time that I personally would like to meet your princess."

James smiles widely so that both of his dimples clearly show. "Easier said than done, Satori. No offense to you personally, but Cinda will want no part of meeting you or of making any changes in herself. She is certain that everything is my fault and has nothing to do with her. She thinks that I distort what I tell you about her."

Satori's gaze is unwavering. "I have heard these reasons many times before. They do not sway me, my son. You have made me quite aware of Cinda's early patterning, but it is important to remember that it is a happy life and loving marriage that Cinda desires and seeks. And at times, it is her fear that speaks more loudly and clearly than her heart. However, we must not let that stop us. Now is the time for us to arrange a meeting with Cinda."

The two men shake hands. Woodrow wags his tail, happy each time he sees James. The prince leaves almost in a run, feeling stronger, proudly going over his first major accomplishment with Cinda.

Questions:

Have you noticed that PERSISTENTLY changing the way you react to others causes them to change the way they react to you— even though it gets worse at first?

16

Cinda Meets Satori and Faces Her Past

*J*ames finally works up the courage to ask Cinda to join him. After much persuasion and many tears, Cinda is seated with James across from the wise and kindly sage. She agrees to meet him partly out of curiosity and partly because she secretly worries that James has shared too much of their lives with him.

Once Cinda actually meets Satori, she hides her surprise and excitement. She feels an immediate liking for him, in spite of herself. However, past experience has taught her to be wary, and she will not let her guard down easily. Cinda takes care to appear less than impressed and rather skeptical of Satori. She suspiciously asks James, "How is this man going to help us?" Her cynical attitude is part of a well-honed practice Cinda has used for many years to hide her fears.

James ignores her words in an effort to stop them from hurting him.

Satori seeks to reassure the couple. "My children, I am here to help you. If indeed you wish to save your marriage, you will need to develop the ability to compromise and, most of all, the courage to argue by truly listening and hearing each other's opposite point of view."

> If indeed you wish to save your marriage, you will need to develop the ability to compromise and, most of all, the courage to argue by truly listening and hearing each other's opposite point of view.

Cinda is aware as her body tenses. She is prepared for Satori to take James's side. But as he speaks to both of them kindly and shows no preference, Cinda slowly responds to the powers of this man's wise and gentle nature. She relaxes a bit and begins to believe that he is indeed an unusual person.

James gazes into Cinda's eyes, realizing that Satori is getting through to his princess. He hopes to learn how he can do the same. Cinda also notices the respect James has for this man. She decides that she will watch and listen. Perhaps the way this man speaks to James may be valuable for her to learn. She really does not want to lose her husband's love. Cinda tentatively wonders if this could be the answer to her prayers.

James, although embarrassed, expresses his feelings quite openly. "We have the courage to argue, but I don't remember either of us having the ability to listen."

"Yes, at least we are experts at arguing with each other. So I guess we are cured—let's go," Cinda adds flippantly with a forced smile.

Satori and James also smile briefly, glad for some relief of the tension, however slight.

"Good, Cinda," Satori says warmly. "Having a sense of humor is essential. To help us get started, I would like you to tell me your feelings in this marriage."

Cinda shifts in her seat and leans forward. She is glad to go first so that this man can know her side of the battle. Satori is enchanted by her captivating smile and manner as she says, "This is all very interesting. But James rarely listens to me. When he disagrees, rather than express his point of view, he simply gets up and leaves, only to hold it in and yell and scream about it later. This infuriates me! When I do tell him how I feel, he doesn't really listen at all. It's James who needs the courage to listen and not ignore what I say.

"Because I'm afraid of his reaction, I also hold my feelings in day after day, and when I finally do express myself, I yell, scream, rant, and rave. I'll do anything to be heard even when that seems to get me nowhere." Cinda breathes out quickly, surprised at her own candor.

Satori looks at her sympathetically. "I can understand how difficult that is for you ..."

Cinda interrupts, no longer smiling, "But you see, no one can talk to James. When he doesn't like what he is hearing, he walks away. Then what am I supposed to do?"

"Thank you for asking, dear. Sometimes, one does not respond to what the other is saying—not because of the words—but because of the tone of voice that one uses. Cinda, may I ask you to heed one lesson before James and you can begin to talk and listen?"

Cinda thinks, *Here it comes, more criticism, as usual.* She fights the urge to bolt because she feels compelled to hear more. She nods doubtfully.

Satori continues, "I understand your resentment, and while I would like to help, it is important that you find a loving way to speak to James." Knowing that Cinda thrives on kind words, as do most people, the wise man adds, "Your sarcasm does not become a girl as sweet and gentle as you. I know you do have a loving voice that once made him listen."

Cinda is taken aback. Impressed by the sage's wisdom and kindness, she begins to desire his approval. "I apologize. I have been holding my feelings in so long, I was not aware of my tone of voice. I will start again."

Inside, Cinda secretly concedes that the sage has made an important point. She had forgotten how bitter she felt when her mother spoke to her in that sarcastic tone of voice. She had not realized that she was doing the same to her prince.

James is filled with admiration. He observes how the holy man speaks firmly but with such kindness that Cinda hears him. He longs to have the same ability.

The sage says, "Let's try again. Are you willing?"

Panic overwhelms Cinda, and in spite of her best intentions, the defensive sarcasm sneaks back into her voice. "I do not believe that after seven years we are just beginning to learn how to speak to each other." Suddenly, she hears her own sarcasm and quickly corrects herself by quietly adding, "But if there is even one chance for us to learn to talk more calmly, how can it hurt? We will still need to talk in reference to our children if we are to divorce." Cinda notices how effortlessly the nastiness slips back into her speech. She had not intended to mention divorce and shamefully notices James's response.

Shivers run down James's spine. Although he is well aware of how unhappy they both are, he had not considered divorce an option. He worries about the effect it could have on their young children, whom they had already hurt so much with their animosity towards one another.

The sage, disregarding Cinda's remarks, looks at James and says, "Quite a smart lady you married."

James smiles, a little perplexed, but quite pleased that this man is able to bring out the best in his princess. He is beginning to feel hope that he may one day be able to recapture the earlier affection he shared with his bride.

Satori turns his calm and steady gaze back to the princess. "Cinda, please look at James and tell him what you are feeling."

James apprehensively turns to face Cinda, though he doesn't look directly at her. He is afraid of the anger that may come out if she speaks so openly. He is convinced it will take a miracle to get the two of them to speak civilly to one another again.

But Cinda gladly continues, again expressing her frustration with James's avoidance of confrontation. "Did you just see his eyes looking to the distance and not towards me? What am I supposed to do?"

The wise man chooses to ignore Cinda's judgment about what she thinks James is feeling. "James, please tell Cinda what you hear her say."

James's brow creases and he asks testily, "Do I have to repeat every word she said?"

Satori is unmoved. "Yes, my son. It is important that you look directly into Cinda's eyes and tell her exactly what you hear." Cinda relaxes as she feels she is finally being heard. She settles back into her chair and looks at James.

Reluctantly, James says, "Fine, I will do my best, but no matter what I say, I know that Cinda will find a way to criticize me. It sounds a bit silly, but I did hear her."

Satori jumps in to encourage his fledgling attempts. "That is exactly the point, my son. You may be hearing all that Cinda says. The question is, does Cinda feel you have heard her?"

Drawing a deep breath, James begins. "I will tell you, Cinda, exactly what I hear." He looks directly into Cinda's eyes. "You are saying no one can talk to me, and when I do not like what I am hearing, I walk away, and you do not know what to do. Did I hear you correctly?"

Cinda nods in affirmation. "Yes, that's right. You just walk away, and I am left to store up my feelings until I can handle them no longer. Then, when I do explode, you leave. My punishment is that I do not see you for days."

James squirms in his chair. He is not embarrassed by what Cinda says but does have some discomfort discussing his deep emotions. He continues to pay close attention to what Cinda is saying and what he thinks she is feeling, but he is not even looking at how he himself responds or how quickly he shies away from criticism. He addresses the sage and ignores his wife. "When Cinda acts like that, the yelling and the hateful tone, I cannot stand it, and then I do feel the need to escape."

Cinda flinches, but she is accustomed to their fights and leans forward so as not to miss a beat. She thinks to herself that Satori must indeed have some unusual powers since James has not yet walked away.

Satori looks from James to Cinda. To keep the conversation flowing, he chooses to refocus them on the task at hand, ignoring their little spat for a moment. "Thank you, James. Would you please summarize what you hear Cinda say?"

James sighs. "You are saying that when I walk away, you are left with stored-up feelings that eventually cause you to explode. Then I punish you by leaving, and you do not see me for days. Is that right, Cinda?"

While Cinda nods in agreement, James wonders, *Can this be true? I go out of my way to hear Cinda's latest misery.*

Cinda believes James does hear her this time, and she sees a glimmer of hope. "Although life seems hopeless now, if James begins to hear me, I know that I will feel much happier."

The sage catches the signs of Cinda's tentative optimism and is quite pleased that she can express such hope at this early stage. "Now, dear Cinda, tell James, 'When you do not listen to me or hear me, it reminds me of when I was a child, and ...'"

Cinda's heart starts pounding, as a bolt of fear runs through her body. She feels the anxiety sweep over her as memories of her childhood come rushing back.

The wise man, sensing Cinda's discomfort, reassures her. "Cinda, my dear, when James hears the feelings you have kept locked inside for all of these years, he will be able to appreciate why you are so upset. Give it a try. If you do not feel somewhat better, I will not ask you such a question again."

Sensing Satori's concern, she lets down her defenses and obeys. With her eyes focused on some inward scene, Cinda takes a deep breath, swallows nervously, and addresses James. "When you walk away and do not listen to me, it reminds me of when I was a child, and ..." Cinda pauses, her unshed tears choking her.

"Go on, my dear. Tell James what it reminds you of," Satori gently prods.

Clearing her throat, Cinda begins again. "It reminds me of ..." With another burst of emotion, Cinda begins to sob uncontrollably.

Satori pats her arm and hands her a handkerchief. "It is all right, my dear. I can see that when James does not let you know that he hears you, he is triggering strong feelings from your childhood—feelings that have been running your life for all of these years."

Without warning, the eye of the storm appears. Cinda speaks through her tears. "It reminds me of when I was little, and my mother would never listen to me. She would act as if I wasn't there, and I would be scared that she would leave me and never come back ... like ... like Daddy."

At that moment, James sees the girl he married. As she speaks her true feelings without sarcasm or anger, James's heart goes out to her as it once did seven years ago. "Cinda, it is your sweet, gentle tone of voice that makes me want to reach out to you. I have not seen you like this since our wonderful first year of marriage."

The sage smiles as he is in approval of James's courage. However, he is intent upon completing his work. "Why were you frightened that your mother would leave and never return, my child?"

Cinda answers matter-of-factly, "Because she told me, 'I am going to leave you and never come back, just like daddy did.' I believed her because she was right. Daddy left and never did come back."

James softly says, "Now I understand the fear I feel coming from you each morning as I leave for my day. It is not because you want to be critical; your choice to be critical is coming from your fears. I had not realized why you react the way you do until now."

The holy man looks at James with a knowing eye. He says, "Cinda, now tell James what you feel when he appears to not listen and walks away."

Cinda continues to sob and looks directly into James's eyes. "It is true. I am scared that you are going to leave—just like Daddy. He said he would come back for me, but he never did. Mommy kept telling me she would leave, too. I was terrified that she would not be there either when I came home from school."

This is a new beginning.

James, with love in his voice and tears in his eyes, repeats all Cinda has said. "Is there more?"

The wise man asks James to put himself in Cinda's shoes and tell her what it would feel like for him if he experienced her terror as a child.

James answers, "Cinda, if I lived every day in fear that my mother would leave me alone just like my father did, I, too, would be anxious and apprehensive if you walked away from me without listening or telling me where you were going."

Cinda sniffles, and James spontaneously reaches out and hugs her. She feels relief and believes that James really understands for the very first time how she feels.

The sage is also pleased. "There is much work ahead, but this is a good beginning. Do you agree?"

They nod, and James says, "My darling, I do not want to leave you feeling scared and alone. Should I tell you why I run away and do not listen to you?"

Cinda brushes tears from her eyes. "Yes, tell me."

James says, "When you run after me in such a panic and tell me what I do wrong, I feel like a little boy being punished by Mother. That is why I run away."

The wise man asks Cinda to tell James what she hears. As she does so, Cinda, too, understands for the first time. She sees this as a truly good beginning. Cinda is surprised to hear her voice promising to return.

As he walks back to the castle, James thinks, *This is a new beginning.*

In his study, Satori thinks, "I am grateful Cinda and James are ready to enter the Cooperation Stage of Marriage."

Questions:
What do you remember about the way your parents treated you?

17

James and Cinda Make Progress

*I*ntrigued by their first meeting and feeling a spark of hope, Cinda agrees to accompany James to another meeting with Satori.

Satori begins by commending both of them on their courage and perseverance. After briefly summarizing what happened at the last meeting, he decides they should begin with James.

James starts by saying, "Cinda, when you talk to me in a sarcastic tone, I do not feel close to you."

Now it is Cinda's turn to mirror James, but still afraid of criticism, she balks and attempts to redirect their focus by casting doubt on the methods. "Satori, with all due respect, I truly do not understand why you ask me to tell James what I hear him say. How silly! Why bother to repeat what he says? We're not in kindergarten."

Satori, the philosopher, mentor, and coach, clearly understands the reasons for Cinda's question but wisely ignores it. "My child, if you think about what I am asking, you will understand. You told James how you felt last time, and James heard your words. You did not believe that he truly cared about your feelings until he put himself in your shoes and repeated to you in his own words what he heard you say. Is that not so?"

Cinda, giving in a bit, says, "Yes. I do not think James hears me, and I do not believe he understands my feelings at all, but when he repeated them to me and put himself in my life, I did feel he understood."

"Thank you, my dear," Satori replies. "That is the value of the practice of telling your partner exactly what you hear him say. Do not forget that each of you has different perceptions of the very same words; your ideas and feelings about what you hear are firmly entrenched in the way you were raised.

"For example, Cinda, do you know why James doesn't feel close to you when you speak to him with a sarcastic tone?"

Cinda glances at James. "I have no idea."

Satori says, "Exactly my point. By mirroring each other's words, you begin to understand what prevents closeness. Authentic communication is a valuable process. As you are quite intelligent, indeed, you will catch on quickly."

Again, James sees the value of commenting on Cinda's positive traits and how it relaxes his princess.

"Please, child, look James in the eye and ask him this very question."

Cinda resents being told what to do, but as she fidgets in her chair, she makes a quick decision to listen to Satori and try. "James, what do you really mean when you speak of my sarcastic tone?"

James begins, "I do not enjoy being spoken to in a critical and condescending tone of voice ..."

Satori interrupts. "James, I wish to ask you to repeat what you said to Cinda, but then add the following sentence: 'It reminds me of when I was a child, and ...'"

James, uneasy but glad to do what Satori asks, looks directly into Cinda's beautiful blue eyes. "It reminds me of when I was a child and ..." Tears begin to form as James remembers. "It reminds me of when I was a child and ..." James pauses, "... all I ever heard was my father's criticism of me."

Cinda is astonished to hear what she never would have guessed. Her heart goes out to James, as she too remembers her mother's unending criticism. Cinda mirrors, summarizes, and empathizes by putting herself in James's shoes. There is a deep silence at the end, both feeling understood for the first time in years. She sees in James the gallant prince she married so long ago.

Satori smiles encouragingly at Cinda. "That was excellent, Cinda. You indeed learn quickly. You have aptly illustrated to me what I have grown to understand about relationships—the reason why two people attract each other beyond even the chemistry that brings them together ..."

Cinda and James share a puzzled look as they wait to hear Satori elaborate on his cryptic thought.

"You have shown that each of you carry the same childhood wound of criticism. Soon, you will also discover that you handle your wounds in opposite ways. This difference may seem small, but it is not. It is the essence of your attraction. When you understand why you react as you do, you will be beginning the process of learning to know thyself, which will make all of the difference."

Cinda frowns, doubt creeping back into her thoughts. "Are you saying that I am attracted to James because he criticizes me?"

"No, my dear. You have watched James from the very first moment you met; his handling of criticism is quite opposite yours. But as of yet, you do not understand how helpful it is. There is a part of you underlying your feelings called your unconscious self, and this part knows all. When you begin to know this part of yourself, you will begin to understand why you react as you do to each other."

> There is a part of you underlying your feelings called your unconscious self, and this part knows all.

Cinda, still confused, asks, "How will this help us?"

"My child, it will put you in control of your life as it is today. For now, the only clue you have in knowing yourself appears in the night when you dream. At that time, you are the producer and director of your dreams, as all of your wishes and fears, which are brought together during the time you are sleeping, tell all."

Cinda exclaims, "I have such awful nightmares that I wake up in a fury—sometimes afraid to go back to sleep."

"And what, my child," Satori asks, "appears mostly in your dreams?"

Cinda pauses as she remembers. "I am always scared, and I'm running away from something or someone. When

I awoke this morning, I realized the person in my dream that scared me was just like my mother."

Satori nods. "You see, my child, when you think of the events in your dreams, you will see that they can be about what happened yesterday, or even many years before. They come together at night when you sleep and are less on guard."

Cinda's eyes widen. "You may be right. I just saw my mother yesterday and that awful nightmare was last night."

"Yes, my dear, your unconscious mind remembers events from your past, but you push them away during daylight. As a survival mechanism, they appear in your dreams at night, many times after you meet a person or encounter an event that brings them to mind."

Cinda, her curiosity sparked, is interested in learning more. James is pleased, but he impatiently shifts in the chair. He is tired of sharing the spotlight with Cinda, even though he has wanted to include her in his meetings with Satori.

Satori notices James's impatience. "James, we will get back to you. The point I am making is that your unconscious self feels attracted to someone who understands your wounds very deeply but reacts in the opposite way. While your first attraction to each other is romantic, after much time passes, the frustrations and struggles you face are quite a normal part of trying to get your needs met. Since you handle your wounds in opposite ways, you are brought together to learn from each other. With knowledge and understanding, you can become each other's healer."

James says, "It seems quite complicated, Satori, but I trust your wisdom. I have already experienced the many benefits from what you have taught me."

"Thank you, James. I have learned this truth by observing and talking to the many couples who have come to me in the past. I have learned that those who have had the perseverance to become aware of their unconscious agendas and have developed the skills needed in relationships have benefited greatly, both as a couple and as individuals. Finding a deeper, more lasting love is not an easy challenge and is meant only for those brave and hearty of spirit.

"Now, back to the task at hand. You are taking your first steps towards learning to get through the frustrations and struggles you now face together. James, perhaps you can repeat what you were saying to Cinda, and Cinda can mirror your feelings."

James gladly agrees. "You see, Cinda, I have had so much blame and criticism in my lifetime that I have taught myself to immediately block out negative words—especially from you."

Cinda mirrors James's words but stumbles at his "especially from you" comment.

Satori explains, "Because James loves you so and chose you as his partner, Cinda, your criticism triggers unconscious angry feelings towards his father or his mother. You, too, have transferred the same unconscious angry feelings you feel towards your parents onto James. When you become aware of your perceptions that are influenced by your childhood experiences, you will begin to see the real person you married, without the encumbrance of parents' deficiencies.

"Because both of you are unaware of the negative feelings you trigger in each other, your struggle to communicate, although a natural part of marriage, is difficult. When you learn how to put your angry feelings in the past and allow your wounds from criticism to heal, the good feelings you have towards each other will come to the surface once again. This process will put you in charge of your feelings, rather than your feelings in charge of you—as is the case now. In other words, you can become the captain of your ship, responsible for all you say and do."

Questions:
What aspects of Satori's personality help Cinda to feel loved and secure?

What aspects of your partner's personality help you to feel loved and secure?

18

The Work Continues and More Hidden Feelings Surface

The meeting is far from over. While Cinda and James are making progress, there is still much work to do. In spite of the difficulties, both are eager to continue as they begin to leave the Rebellious Stage of marriage behind.

Cinda is still mirroring and empathizing with James, when unexpectedly, she asks him, "Is there more you would like to share?" She is surprised when James replies, "Yes." He has not told her any of his feelings in a long time, and her normally taciturn prince seems to have so much to say.

James clears his throat and continues. "When you talk to me in a demeaning tone, I feel like I am a child again, being shamed by my father." Cinda mirrors James, and he starts again. "I promised myself that I would never again live in the same negative environment my parents shared. The worst part for me was watching Mother being criticized mercilessly by Father. She didn't do anything about it, but I intend to."

Cinda realizes that she has not thought about James's feelings lately, having been consumed by her own. She finally concedes that Satori may have something to offer them, and she does not have all the answers.

Satori smiles at James. "I see this process has given you the courage to speak your truth."

James returns his smile. "You are right, Satori. I never talked about it before because I didn't feel like she listened to me."

Satori looks at Cinda and waits until she meets his eyes to speak. "Cinda, your work from here forward depends upon understanding what James has just said. You see, by telling him all that you hear, even though you may not agree or even see its importance, you are opening the doorway to communication—a very important step. You are now building the neces-

> You are now building the necessary and strong foundation that helps relationships thrive.

sary and strong foundation that helps relationships thrive. Understand, you will have your turn to disagree, but in all fairness, you must wait until James is finished, just as he must allow you your time to speak and be heard."

Cinda, now feeling grateful for Satori's help, willingly mirrors and summarizes what James says. When it is her turn to empathize, she says, "James, I do know how much criticism hurts you; I see it in your face. And it is true that when you hear criticism, you walk away because you believe words can destroy you. I see Satori's point because I have learned to be critical in order to prevent criticism from being leveled at me. It looks as though we do handle our childhood wounds in opposite ways."

Satori nods at the couple. "Once again, I am quite pleased, Cinda. You have already learned a great deal. Can you now see that mirroring prevents each of you from interpreting what the other means?"

"Yes," she says, "when I mirror James, I actually stop assuming what he means. It seems I have been wrong all along."

"When assumptions seep in, you hear words, but you cannot truly realize what is being said. Since this concept is so critical to your happiness, I would like you, too, James, to mirror what is being said as it is worth repeating." Satori signals to James to begin.

"I can see when I do not assume what Cinda means and I mirror her words, I will actually hear and learn from her opposite point of view."

Satori looks approvingly at his two pupils. "Yes, my children. I am teaching you not to read minds but instead to listen and ask so that you can hear truth. That alone will help you understand what is said and help you not to take your partner's words personally. For the words you hear are not about you, but about your partner's very own feelings."

James leans forward, listening intently. "Satori, I can see that it's difficult for most of us to avoid putting our own feelings into what we hear, even though we are not children anymore. Those habits we developed as children don't work for us as adults."

"Yes, that is the reason I am asking you to learn the process of mirroring the other. This helps you to not confuse the issue by personalizing what you are hearing.

"Personalizing, simply put, causes a never-ending round of fights. When you follow my instructions and mirror back the other's words, you will know exactly what is meant. Only then will you be able to respond to what is actually said and not to your own perception of what you think is meant. You will hear that what is said is not about you, but about your partner's feelings and perceptions."

Cinda frowns slightly. She says slowly, "It is hard for me to believe that what James says has little to do with me."

The wise man understands her confusion. "It is a difficult concept, my child. What James says may be his reaction to what you say and the feelings it triggers within him, but what is happening is not about you. It is about him. Do I make sense to you, my child?"

Cinda finds herself unable to remain angry with Satori. She does not remember anyone ever speaking to her in such an understanding way. She wonders, *Could James be right about my tone of voice?*

Cinda, committing herself further to the process, asks Satori another question, for the first time with trust in her heart. "Satori, what should I do when I feel James is directly criticizing me, even though you tell me it is not personal?"

"An excellent question, my child. You must calm the little girl inside you who has always been criticized. Tell Little Cinda that James is not talking about her, although it does sound that way. Then take several deep breaths, even leave the room to calm yourself. Tell James you will be back in a few moments, as it may be the perfect time to take a break. When you feel agitated, I encourage you to take a few moments to listen to your feelings. Close your eyes and go deep within—to your heart. This is a very ancient method of healing."

Satori continues, "When James's words or actions rile you, my child, it is your cue that he is triggering a feeling within you that originated in your past. It is helpful to write your angry reactions in your diary and sleep on them. The next day, write your feelings again and then request a dialogue. The ultimate problem you face is to begin to trust that James is not intentionally trying to hurt you."

Cinda's frown is gone and her expression lightens. "I understand. When I am upset, I have to trust my feelings and not see the worst in James, but uncover the reason why my anger has been triggered."

Satori claps his hands together. "Yes, exactly so! As you learn to trust yourself, you will trust James for who he is, and he will begin to respond in kind."

As Cinda pauses to reflect upon his wisdom, Satori notices James fidgeting. "Before ending today, James, is there any sentence in your dialogue that Cinda did not mirror to you?"

James loosens the top button of his shirt. "Yes, there is. Cinda, when you talk to me in a sarcastic and demeaning tone of voice, I feel emasculated, and then sex is the last thing on my mind."

Although surprised, Cinda hears James clearly for the first time. She is astounded to discover the real reason for James's apparent rejection. Morella had been telling her it was her looks. Cinda plans to relay this information, thinking Morella will be pleased for her. Cinda contemplates what James just said. *James's lack of sexual desire is not about my looks or because he is cheating on me with another more attractive woman. It is about my demeanor. What a relief!* Her faith in the process begins to build, and she mirrors James's words.

There is hope in the air as James and Cinda take their leave. Woodrow leaps up and kisses both of them. Satori muses: *Although it will take some time for each to truly leave the Rebellious Stage of their marriage behind, I have confidence that they are beginning to do so. Although there is much work ahead—the groundwork has been laid.* He quickly looks up as Cinda interrupts his thought. "Satori, you have such a lovable companion. Woodrow, I will see you again soon."

Questions:
How can you see that mirroring what the other person says helps you to truly understand what he/she means?

19

Satori Wins Cinda Over

$\mathcal{T}$hat night, Cinda has a vivid dream. She is riding a white horse, dressed in a magnificent gown the color of dark sapphires, and wearing a queen's crown upon her head. James rides beside her on a black horse. He is also magnificently arrayed in a red robe with an ermine hem. Leading the horses is none other than Satori, who looks back at them with a twinkle in his eye. This dream vanishes from her memory, but the mood of the dream lingers as she slowly opens her eyes.

It is only 6:00 a.m., and dawn has barely crept into the sky, but the princess, who usually does not arise from bed until the children are awake, jumps up, excited to meet with Satori again. She begins by shaking James, snug in his bed, telling him to get dressed so they can get on with their journey to meet Satori.

Walking to their session, they are aware they are not holding hands—a habit long ago abandoned.

When the session begins, Satori goes right to the heart of the matter. "Yesterday's session was quite promising, and I have been looking forward to continuing."

James and Cinda smile and simultaneously say, "Me too." Amazed, they look at each other and laugh.

Satori also laughs. "My children, you have just shown me that you are both on the same spiritual wave, by thinking the same thoughts. Synchronicity is another good sign. Now, before we proceed any further, may I ask if it is true that you two have been unhappy for nearly seven years?"

James and Cinda nod in agreement, glancing at each other nervously. Satori says, "I am certain after seven years of unhappiness you can handle three more months of solid work together for the sake of your marriage. Is this true?"

James, instead of answering for himself, turns to his wife and asks, "Are you willing to commit to three months with Satori, Cinda?"

Cinda, with a tremor of panic in her voice, addresses Satori instead of answering James. "What are you talking about? That is far too many sessions. You know I don't have that kind of time to spare."

James observes Satori trying hard to restrain himself as he speaks in somewhat controlled bewilderment. "To heal a marriage and change the lives of you and your children? It is hardly enough time! What else could be more important than your happiness?"

Cinda twists her hands in her lap. "Do I have a guarantee, Satori?" Then, in a more sober tone, she corrects herself. "I realize there is none. If only for the sake of our children, I agree we must do as much as we can to bring our marriage together. But what if this isn't possible?"

"My dear, as long as you are willing to commit to demonstrating integrity towards yourself—and that means keeping your word to yourself—anything is possible. However, if you do keep your words to yourselves, and you are no happier in three months and see no hope, then it is only fair that you part ways."

"You mean that if we cannot find happiness and love again, after we travel the extra mile to do what we must, then it is better to part?" James asks with a look of astonishment.

Satori nods slowly. "Yes, my son. You will be learning how to alter your childhood conditioning by responding positively towards each other, rather than the way you were raised. There is no better gift to give to your children than positive modeling. To have integrity means to keep the commitment you make to yourself, no matter how hard it gets or difficult it becomes."

Cinda smiles timidly. "Well, Satori, if you are talking about me knowing how to keep promises to myself, then I can assuredly tell you I will do so."

James feels a surge of optimism and smiles broadly. "I will keep my promises to myself no matter how hard it gets or how difficult it becomes. I owe integrity to Cinda, our children, our kingdom, and most of all to myself."

Satori reaches out and squeezes both of their hands. "Excellent. Then an agreement is made. Part two of your journey is about to begin. I'm requesting that the thought or even mention of divorce or separation is put on hold for three months. Will you also agree to that?"

Together, James and Cinda give their assurances, while Satori inwardly muses, 'I shall call this the Cooperation Phase.'

Questions:
What value does committing to learning how to understand and communicate with each other have for you and your relationship?

What excuses do you use to avoid taking responsibility?

20

James and Cinda Learn about Commitment

In their next meeting, Satori reiterates the importance of integrity. "My children, let us reaffirm what we have said about integrity so that there will be no misinterpretation. Integrity is your first commitment to yourself. While I expect you to give your best to your work together, I also ask that you each do what is needed to find your own happiness."

Cinda understands the idea about taking care of herself first, as it was what she did in order to survive her childhood. She glances over at James, whose brow is furrowed in evident confusion. "Why do we commit to ourselves first? Aren't I supposed to be committed to Cinda and our children first and only then to myself?" he asks.

Satori shakes his head. "Experience has taught me that when I ask couples to keep commitments to each other, they at first say 'yes,' but upon leaving my quarters, practice 'no.' Therefore, by making your first commitment to yourself and your own integrity, you begin to take ownership of your happiness. As you must live with yourself forever, there can be no parting of the ways. This underlies the importance of the phrase, 'To thine own self be true.'"

Cinda wants to make sure she has heard correctly. "Does that mean that if I make a promise to respond in a certain way to James, I am promising myself and not James?"

Satori nods. "Exactly, my dear. That way, you have no one to blame but yourself when you do not follow through with your commitment."

Cinda narrows her eyes a bit as she replies, "I remember my parents used to make many promises to each other, but I never saw them keep any of them. This will be difficult for me. What comes first—changing patterns or making commitments?"

"A good question, indeed. It will take time to change patterns, as they have been longtime parts of your life. Accomplishing both at the same time will be difficult. These changes will be works in progress. Please remember that you will make mistakes. Remember, 'To err is human, to forgive is divine.' Therefore, I am asking you to see your mistakes as if you are another person. That means to step outside yourselves, view your mistakes, and then begin understanding them, without criticism. Understanding and accepting why you do what you do will make all of the difference in becoming aware of your behavior and then changing it. This will lead to acceptance of your entire self, both the negative and positive parts."

James asks, "Are you asking us to notice our mistakes, but not criticize ourselves or each other for making them?"

Cinda looks down, knowing that James is speaking of her, and in a sincere moment of weakness, acknowledges her own behavior.

James, realizing the accusation present in his own remarks, adds in a conciliatory tone, "I can see how difficult it will be for both of us. I have heard nothing but blame, shame, and criticism all of my life. I have a lot of work to do in this area. I'm constantly criticizing myself."

Satori nods. "Yes, my children, letting go of criticism is a top priority in this family. I am asking that when you notice your own mistakes, learn not to be critical of them. Instead, decide what you need to learn in order to correct them from here on. By doing this, you will be taking your first step towards changing your patterns. That is how you begin to create a new life, devoid of negativity—for you and your children, as well as those in the kingdom you will one day rule."

James breathes a sigh of relief and happiness. "Thank you, Satori. My greatest desire is to help myself, my wife and children, and the people of my kingdom."

"I know this to be true—that is the reason I am here. Cinda, is it true that you, too, care for the people in the kingdom?"

Cinda thinks for a moment. "Honestly, I do. But for now, I have so much work to do myself that it will be a long time before I can help others. My first priority is our family."

"I know this, also, to be true, my dear," Satori says. "The kingdom will benefit from your efforts; it is a difficult task, but it will be life changing. However, it is important I inform you that while I can communicate my wisdom, you are the ones who must live what we speak in order to find happiness for yourselves. Although what I say appears simple, it is quite another matter to live by your words—and to find your own truth."

The sage stops to think for a moment and then looks directly at Cinda and James. "Before we continue, my children, I have a request. Would each of you promise that what is said in this room stays in this room, and you will not speak of these words when you are at home?"

Cinda's mouth drops open in shock. "Why? James is my husband. I can say anything I want to him."

The wise man explains. "Cinda, if James were to laugh at your tears when at home, or tell you that you were being overly dramatic, how would you feel?"

Cinda sputters indignantly. "Why, you better believe that I would never express my feelings again to James, either here or at home."

"Yes, my dear, and you would be correct. After all, you alone must keep yourself feeling safe. Is that not true, my dear?"

Cinda's eyes well with tears and she nods in agreement.

Satori continues, "If the feelings you express here are thrown at you when at home, you will not feel safe, thus defeating your purpose for being here. Do you understand, my dear?"

Cinda sighs and again nods in the affirmative, as does James.

"It is most important to help you understand that when you say anything you wish, even in anger, you lack sensitivity to your partner's feelings, and neither of you feel safe in speaking to the other again because your childhood wounds have been reopened."

Satori clears his throat and looks at both of them steadily. "My children, it is never right to say whatever you want and disregard the other's feelings. You must respect them as your own; only then can happiness grow." They both listen intently to Satori, not looking at each other.

> When you feel safe expressing your deepest feelings, you are taking your first step towards bringing love lost back into your lives.

"When you feel safe expressing your deepest feelings, you are taking your first step towards bringing love lost back into your lives."

Cinda and James turn and look deeply into one another's eyes and, for the first time this evening, hold each other's gaze without turning away. "I promise I won't speak of my darkest feelings outside these walls until we have learned to communicate safely."

Cinda looks back at James. "I promise, too."

The wise man smiles proudly. "My children, you have just made your first commitment to yourselves today and have set boundaries of safety. In time, you will learn how to transfer the knowledge you gain in this room to your home and speak openly and freely of your deepest feelings without fear of reprisal. Please be aware that this means that when you leave here, both of you are never to use what was said here against each other—especially in a fit of anger or to get even. Keeping this commitment will allow you to feel safe enough to discover the wounds and fears from childhood that are still driving your behavior today."

James smiles lovingly at Cinda. "I will keep my promise."

Cinda nods and smiles back. She is relieved and trusts James for the first time in years.

Questions:
How does committing to integrity to yourself help you to feel safe in expressing your feelings?

How can you learn to practice more assertive communication rather than aggressive or passive communication?

21

A Light Appears on the Horizon

*A*t home that evening, Cinda says to James with a note of hope in her voice, "It seems there is a whole new way of life awaiting us. Commitment to self is quite an astounding concept. Do you think it's really possible to incorporate these methods into our lives? You know they'll be more difficult than Satori describes."

James agrees. "That's true. We should ask Satori about it tomorrow."

Bright and early the next morning, James asks Cinda if she would like to walk with him. Cinda smiles and replies, "Yes, James, I would like to—as long as we don't talk about any subject that triggers childhood feelings within us. I want to be able to keep my promise."

Although James is eager to do more, he relents, understanding Cinda's discomfort. "That's fine, but can we also agree to practice summarizing, talking to each other, hearing what was said, and repeating it back? This is the homework Satori has encouraged which we have shied away from."

Cinda, afraid of failing, objects. "It's going to take time for us to practice what we are learning. For now, let's just absorb it all as that is difficult enough. Satori once told me, 'One thing at a time and that done well.' Our second step will be practice. Okay? We will get there, but let's be patient."

James thoughtfully responds, "It's rather nice to hear you speak of patience, Cinda. My parents never heard of patience. Did yours?" They both laugh, relieved to be able to agree on something.

At their next meeting with Satori, Cinda begins immediately. "Satori, James and I are having a difficult time putting into practice all that you have been teaching us."

"Let me try to make it more practical," Satori says. "You may have heard of the concept of being at one with what you are doing. Let us take the sport of fencing for an example. You will be able to excel in that sport when you and the sword feel as if you are one with each other. Or as a painter, you will truly express yourself only if you are one with the brush. The same concept applies to this task. There is a little child inside each of you. That is the child you have been speaking of, Cinda—the one your mother never listened to and James does not hear either. In order to help Little Cinda, your first step will be to be patient with James and tell Little Cinda that James is trying, but he does not always remember. He, too, has a wound that prevents him from hearing you. As he becomes aware of how he is reacting, he will be more attentive to you. In the meantime, you must calm Little Cinda and begin to trust that you will accomplish what you believe you can. You must become the mother Little Cinda never had."

Cinda's new awareness tells her that Satori speaks from wisdom, so she spends the afternoon mulling over this idea, determined to apply it to her life.

Later that night, James is astonished to hear Cinda say, "When I learn to be the mother to Little Cinda that I never had, I'm sure I can also be the mother to Luke and Lucinda that I always wanted to be."

James and Cinda have a wonderful evening, the first in a long time, but the trouble is far from over. The arduous journey is just beginning.

Questions:

When have you been able to find the little child in you and let your child know that you, the adult, are there for little you?

What does your little child need from you in order to feel safe, secure, and empowered?

22

Morella Strikes

*A*fter several satisfying and challenging meetings with Satori, life for the royal couple begins to settle into a calm, peaceful routine. Cinda feels more content and cannot stop herself from thinking about the happiness she can achieve in herself and in her marriage. She is looking forward to the upcoming ball and feels proud to be a part of the royal family.

One day, she finds lipstick on James's shirt. When she asks James, he laughs as he tells her, "Lucinda had been playing with your lipstick. I didn't realize that some had gotten on my shirt when I hugged her last night."

Cinda accepts James's explanation. She is even pleased that he is so attentive to his daughter.

Morella responds quite differently when Cinda relates the event to her. "Have you lost your mind? Do you really think James is different from your father? He is a man, isn't he? I remember what your mother told us about men, even if you don't."

After hearing these words from her dearest friend, the old feelings of mistrust begin to return to Cinda. She comforts herself with the thought that the wise sage believes in James. She tries to convince herself that she does as well. But Morella's poisonous words have hit their mark, drawing up Cinda's fears once again. Cinda even begins to wonder whether she should trust Satori. The distrust and suspicion with which she was raised prompt her to question herself and all those she loves, so afraid is she that she may be hurt or abandoned.

Sensing Cinda's wavering trust, Morella fans the flames. "Do you know what James does when he goes on his trips? Last month, he brought you a beautiful white Lipizzaner horse, didn't he? Why do you think he did this? Perhaps he is covering something."

Cinda immediately feels old fears come to the surface. "Is it possible I have been blind? Is James having an affair?"

Morella pretends to be disappointed and sad for her friend. She treacherously repeats the words Cinda's mother had often uttered, "Men, they can't be trusted."

Later that evening, Cinda speaks to James, but this time with the old, suspicious, nagging voice. As she pours an after-dinner liqueur into his glass, she says, "Oh, I see there is no lipstick on your shirt today, my dear."

James becomes angry at her words, unaware of why, until he voices his feelings to himself as Satori had suggested. When he asks, "What is it that makes me wary?" the answer comes, "It is that old distrustful voice of Cinda's returning once again. I can recognize it anywhere."

Although he has recognized the problem, James doesn't choose his new enlightened path of communicating with Cinda; he too reverts back to his old ways, still unable to confront her. He stalks off in the opposite direction, leaving his glass untouched, and avoids his wife for the rest of the evening and most of the next day.

The evening of the ball arrives. The whole kingdom celebrates the wedding anniversary of the queen and king. James decides to put his doubts aside and resolves that he will not allow their most recent quarrels to deprive him of joy tonight.

James arrives handsomely attired in his military uniform. Cinda sees James once again as the handsome, charming prince she had met so long ago and decides, too, to put the lipstick and Morella's warning out of her mind for the evening. Both Cinda and James look superb as they dance to their favorite waltz, peering into one another's eyes with the love they once felt seven years ago. Morella watches with a dark glee as she plots her friend's downfall.

The palace is overflowing with food, wine, music, and festivities. The ballroom is filled with hundreds of guests. While dancing with Cinda, out of the corner of his eye, James catches a glimpse of a black-cloaked man standing in the shadows of the darkest part of the room. The dance ends, and just as he is about to approach the man, Morella interrupts and offers her arm for a dance with him. Unaware of her motives, James willingly obliges.

After a lovely dance, Morella takes James aside. "Your Highness, in all sincerity, I must inform you that Cinda has recently told me that the magnificent, imperial white

Lipizzaner horse you imported from Austria, your devas-
tatingly expensive gift to her last month, was just a means
for you to cover your own guilt."

He is shocked into anger. "What guilt?" he says, now
focused on his anger and forgetting about the man in the
dark shadows.

"Why, your princess is certain you were sleeping with
another woman," Morella hisses. She darts away, having
thrust her poison into his mind like a snake.

When, at that moment, Cinda arrives and asks her
husband for a dance, James's fury is beyond restraint, and
he loses all control of himself.

"My dearest princess, I must tell you that I traveled
across the continent to have the Lipizzaner horse sent to
you, the finest one I have seen, as a token of my love. And
you, with your twisted mind, view it as me feeling guilty
because you think I have been cheating on you—sleeping with another woman? If that were true—although it
is not—why shouldn't I? What affections do you return to
me, even now during our work with Satori? We can't even
have warm, loving conversation because of your fears. It
seems that your sick mind will not be cured. Your lack of
belief in yourself accompanied by your acquired ability to
blame others keeps you in misery.

"I have stayed with you because of my principles. Yes,
my dear, I do have integrity—unlike the father who raised
you. I have no reason to sneak behind your back. I am a
prince—soon to be a king. The woman at my side must be
able to have trust and appreciation for who I am and the
work I plan for my kingdom. I cannot afford to bring my

life down to the gutters of distrust. It is too lowly for the ruler of a kingdom. I have pledged to uphold my integrity and my values for the good of our children, my kingdom, and myself, and that is what I will do. For your own sake, pull your mind away from jealousy, hate, anger, and mistrust. I will not abide that in the woman at my side."

Cinda listens, trembling, and unable to utter a word. She cannot imagine what set James off.

James, although miserable as his powerful anger begins to fade, continues to speak proudly in his own defense. He knows Cinda's trust has been misplaced. It makes him even angrier that she would trust someone as blatantly scheming as Morella, but not trust her own husband. "You speak so highly of your trusted friend, Morella. What a fool you are! Ask her if I have turned down her affections so willingly offered. She, too, wants to be a princess. Not for me! My princess has to have beauty on the inside as well as on the outside. Your loyalties are dangerously misplaced." James stalks off and does not look in Cinda's direction.

Queen Elayna is nearby, witnessing the whole scene. She does not utter a word but trusts that her son and his wife will find a path to peace. She has great hope that perhaps they will find the understanding that she and the king never achieved. The queen will continue to pray for her son, Cinda, and the children. Nevertheless, she wrings her hands with a feeling of helplessness.

King John has also witnessed the scene. He is solemn, as he feels a deep distress that he dare not consider. He calls for another glass of champagne.

Questions:

How can you determine when the opinions and motives of others are helpful or harmful to your relationship with your partner?

23

Cinda Faces the Painful Truth

*C*inda visits Satori alone the next day and tells him of the events at the ball. Satori is glad that James is no longer lacking in courage, but he is concerned that James continues to communicate aggressively and to say things out of anger that do not necessarily reflect his true feelings towards Cinda. He is also concerned about the fears that this has aroused in Cinda. He tells Cinda, "Now is divine timing for you. My wishes are for you to begin the work that you have been afraid to do until now.

"Cinda, the interaction between the two of you last night holds many lessons for the both of you. Dearest Cinda, why do you give away your power—you who so desperately wants control?"

As Cinda listens, she slowly starts to understand what Satori is saying. She has the hindsight to see how her behavior the night before came out of fear. She knows that behavior that arises from fear prevents her from standing in her power.

Without waiting for an answer, he continues, "You have an important decision to make. Either give up trying to destroy yourself through sabotage and insecurity—just like your parents did—or live with it. The decision is yours to make, as you alone are responsible for you."

Cinda flinches at Satori's firm words. "Satori, you haven't spoken so harshly towards me since we first met. I need to think about what you have said. But I realize that you are right in one thing: If I don't do what it takes to develop trust in myself, I know I will lose all that I have worked so hard to achieve.

> Usually, what we are most angry at in another we find in ourselves.

"When James told me what Morella said to him, I was deeply disturbed. Why would she betray the trust I place in her? She is my one and only trusted friend."

"Cinda, my dear, the one you must trust is yourself, not Morella. You must learn to listen to your own instincts. Has James ever shown himself to be a man who lies and cheats?" Satori hesitates for a moment and then asks, "Or is it you who would lie? Usually, what we are most angry at in another we find in ourselves."

Tears form in Cinda's eyes. She looks sharply at Satori. "You have never spoken such cruel words to me."

Satori does not relent. "When I see you, my child, again discounting who you are by employing your fear which leads to sabotage, after all of your strides, I can do nothing else. I do truly care about you. How can I sit by and watch you give away your power by giving in to fear?"

Cinda looks down at her feet, softening a little. She has never heard such love and firmness in the same moment. In her heart, she knows Satori to be very wise. She asks herself, *Can I rise to the occasion as Satori encourages me to do?* Cinda knows she will have much work to do to discover the real person inside and to find the goodness that resides in there. Her mother told her again and again it was not there. But, Cinda believes that she has much good in her. *Can it be buried deeply inside? I do know in my heart that I am a good person.*

Cinda says quietly, "Satori, I am going home to meditate as you have taught me. I hope to find the truth within myself and then to talk with you again."

"By all means, my dear. While you meditate, hold your hand on your heart and allow the real Cinda to come forward. We will speak again when you are ready."

Questions:

What must you do to prevent a sabotage of your happiness and to develop inner trust?

Do you practice saying what you mean and meaning what you say?

24

James Decides He Can

$\mathcal{S}$atori arranges a session for Cinda and James immediately. They walk in separately. Cinda's eyes are swollen, and the sadness deep within is showing. James asks to speak first. As Cinda does not know what to say, she willingly allows James to go first, hoping to see her apologetic husband once more.

James sits tall; his dark eyes look directly into Cinda's blue eyes. "When you don't trust me, it makes me angry and fearful. I feel as though if you learn how to trust and thereby set boundaries for yourself, our marriage will change. But I fear that without a strong commitment to self, your words will be empty."

Cinda mirrors James's words, as required, and calmly asks, "Is there more?"

James does not break eye contact with Cinda. "Yes, while I continue to love you, I will not accept your treatment of me. I thank you for the love and fun you once brought into my life. But as your husband, I will not accept your negative views anymore."

Cinda flinches at James's harsh words, but she straightens herself in her chair and faces him directly and calmly, determined to meet his criticisms with honesty. "James, I do understand you. I made a commitment to learn to trust myself, and in truth, I am learning to do that. Trusting myself fills me with great fear; I don't want to trust and then be rejected. I do understand that this type of thinking is illogical, and I am working hard to change my feelings."

James mirrors Cinda's words.

Knowing James is listening, Cinda gains confidence. "James, when you yell at me with such anger and force, it causes me to feel fearful and does not allow for us to communicate. I then question not only you, but myself and our commitment to working on our problems. When I'm afraid that our differences will only get worse, I question our ability to overcome our difficulties."

James looks at Cinda with understanding and compassion. He can now see how his anger triggers Cinda's fears and how Cinda's fears trigger his anger. He realizes that in order for the magic to return in their marriage, they will need to work together. He suddenly exclaims, "I can! I won't give up or stop doing what I must—because I can." He stops to take a breath as Cinda looks at him with her brows furrowed. "Cinda, when you believe you can't, you can't! I have heard those words so many times before. For the sake of our happiness, I'm no longer willing to listen. We must choose together, either we will or we will not. We can only be partners when we both have the same mantra by which to live. He slumps over slightly, exhausted by his emotions but also relieved. "Think about it, my dear. If we are willing to live by 'I can' instead of 'I can't,' we can continue to work together with Satori. If we choose otherwise, then I fear our marriage may be over."

> ❧
>
> **We can only be partners when we both have the same mantra by which to live.**
>
> ❧

Cinda is in shock as she contemplates the possibility that James could leave her. She recognizes that he is serious. When they agreed to not discuss the possibility of divorce for three months, Cinda never dreamed it would be James who would break the pact first.

James continues assertively. "As I said, while I still love you, I will not allow myself to stay in a marriage that is unsatisfying or with someone who is unable to commit to making it work."

Cinda cries, "But what about the children!"

James turns abruptly towards Cinda. "The children need honesty and authenticity in their lives, not pretense. It will be painful in the beginning, but they will profit in the end. We can no longer give them such poor examples of parents. Don't you see how their fighting is mimicking our own and also how their fights have grown over the past year? They are suffering with us. If we are apart, perhaps they will be able to heal."

James is unable to stop himself. "It seems to me that our fights must be very similar to those of your parents. Could that possibly be true?"

Cinda looks away, trying to hide the tears that are clouding her eyes. Her response is in a barely audible whisper. "Yes, we are behaving very much like my parents did." This realization sends shivers down Cinda's spine.

She doesn't have to mirror James's words, as he, too, knows she hears them loud and clear. She turns to Satori, who looks at her with kindness and understanding.

"I will return another time. I must leave now." With as much dignity as she can muster, Cinda walks away.

Satori is calm as James begins to speak. "Those were the most difficult words I have ever had to say, Satori. But I meant each one of them. I cannot abide living this way with Cinda anymore."

Satori responds quietly. "There are times when we must be apart before we can be together again. You have kept your commitment to yourself as I have asked, my son. All will show itself in time."

After a long quiet moment, with his index finger on his brow, James says, "I cannot believe that instead of feeling sad and scared as I used to imagine, Satori, I feel strong and free. I am concerned about my marriage to Cinda but have accepted that what must be will be."

"Yes, my son, you are quite right. Your strength will grow as you learn how to be with yourself and free of fear."

"Thank you, Satori; you are a great inspiration and help to me."

Questions:

How does it help you to understand that the ability to be there for yourself will be a catalyst to releasing your fears?

Have you fully committed to working on yourself? Your marriage? To letting go of fear?

25

Cinda Learns to Be True to Herself

*C*inda is sobered by James's words. As she sits by her bedroom window, looking at the beautiful view, she takes a good, hard look at her life. However, when evening comes, she has still not attained enough clarity and serenity to approach James or Satori.

That night, she turns in early, in a secluded extra bedroom at the far end of the castle. Attempting to avoid grappling further with her problems, she takes refuge in sleep, but Cinda cannot escape her dreams.

Little Cinda is seven years old and awaiting the very first birthday party that her mother has finally kept her promise to give. The children are arriving. Cinda dances with excitement; she can hardly wait for the festivities to begin. Her grandparents bring her her own special brown-and-white pony. Cinda thinks, *This is the happiest day of my life.*

The children are gathered around Cinda and everyone is laughing and having a wonderful time. Suddenly, a shrill voice yells, "Sit down! It is time for the birthday cake."

The children immediately stop what they are doing and turn toward the sound of the voice, Cinda's mother. Scared, they run into the back yard. Cinda follows, feeling embarrassed.

Cinda's grandparents ease the tension by beginning a game for the children. They eventually bring everyone into the house, but at the wrong moment. As they are about to sit down for the birthday cake, Cinda's mother again shouts, this time at Cinda's father. "You stupid man! All I asked you to do was to order a cake big enough for ten children and four adults. Look what you brought! There is hardly enough for four of us."

As Cinda's father is about to explain, her mother throws the entire cake into his face. Everyone laughs—especially Morella. Cinda is in tears as she runs after her father. At the top of the stairs, she sees him packing his bags.

Cinda runs to him, her tear-streaked face uplifted to him. Looking down at her, her father says, "Dear Cinda, I cannot spend another moment here with your mother. I am leaving. I promise to come back for you when I have a job and a place to stay." Cinda cries and pleads although she cannot stop her father as he waves goodbye.

The scene switches to Cinda hiding from monsters on a dreary snow-filled day in her dark and cold home. Frightened and unable to find her mother, Cinda runs away from the huge black monster she finds under her bed.

Before Cinda wakes, she sees her father returning to take her with him—only she is seventeen years old.

"Daddy, where have you been? Why haven't you come sooner?"

Her father answers, "I'm a coward. I was afraid to return and face the music."

"What music, Daddy?"

"Why, your mother, of course. I told you that it was her fault I left."

The dream switches to Cinda trying to save her father, who is scared, alone, and shivering in a dreary, dark room.

"No, Cinda, you can't save me—it's too late. I can finally see that all that happened is my fault, not your mother's, as I once told you. My life would be different today if I had stayed. I would stand with pride, having faced your mother and stopped tolerating her constant verbal beatings. Instead, I left and married another woman even worse than your mother. I am running from her now. I'm a coward and a failure. I haven't done anything with my life but blame everybody else."

Cinda awakens in a deep sweat. She jumps out of bed and runs to the woods where she knows Satori will be with his precious dog.

When Cinda arrives, out of breath, she tells him, "Oh, Satori, I have been so wrong. My dream has revealed that James is not at all like my father. I listen and watch James put the children to bed every night. They can't wait to hear their favorite story. I see my James is an honest man."

Satori replies, "For the first time since I have known you, you are crying out for help and reaching towards me, with trust. An awakening is occurring. Go on, my child. What else have you learned?"

"Satori, from watching my family, I know our children feel a genuine commitment from their father. Because Luke and Lucinda still have their father in their lives, they are not losing confidence or trust in themselves, as I did when I was their age.

"My dream revealed that my father, so unlike James, did not have commitment or integrity. The truth that I have been so unwilling to accept has been shown to me. Now I know that before I can ask James to love me again, I must learn to trust myself."

Satori smiles. "Cinda, you have made more progress in one night than many people do in weeks of self-examination. I am proud of you."

Cinda feels a sense of well being, a genuine optimism springing completely from within her own being. She turns to face Satori. "I want to tell James that I believe he has been faithful to me all that time, but I'm afraid. Do you think he will forgive me?"

"I am sure he will, if you speak from your heart," says Satori.

"I hope you're right."

"Remember what I always say, 'To thine own self be true.' If you are true to your own destiny, then all the other relationships in your life will be in harmony, as well."

Cinda sighs. "You make it sound easy, but I know it's not. In many ways, I'm still afraid of trusting James."

"Trust takes time, my child. Could it be that in many ways, you do not trust yourself?"

Cinda sits frozen in time in fear of exposing her true feelings.

Satori continues, "Trust of yourself is your first goal, before you try to trust James. You have years of pain to overcome. Be patient with yourself."

Questions:

How do you take responsibility for your own behavior?

What feelings about your parents and/or your childhood wounds do you project onto your partner?

What are your negative and positive expectations of your partner?

26

Cinda and James Learn to Focus

$\mathcal{T}$ime passes while Cinda and James continue their work separately and together with Satori in hopes of relighting the flames that once brought them together. Although James made great progress early on, Cinda is now readily making strides toward self-awareness as well.

She still has not had the courage to tell James that she now believes in his fidelity. However, in each of their sessions with Satori, she comes closer.

In one session, Cinda says, "Thank you, James, for being so loyal. I really do appreciate your support of me."

James replies, "Thank you, Cinda. I appreciate you and the work you are doing too. I see some hope, Cinda."

During another session when Cinda tells James she still loves him, his heart warms. "I'm also working on trusting my intuition, my own staying positive, and myself," he replies. "Recently, I have realized that by taking responsibility for my actions and my own happiness,

I avoid blaming you for the problems in our marriage. I have found a new powerful way of being."

Cinda and James are beginning to live one day at a time and not project their fears or disappointments onto each other. James meditates a great deal these days, especially when he feels depressed over the emotional distance between himself and Cinda. He knows that it is all in his young family's best interest. Finding a positive way to view his situation and to focus on the progress that has been made eases his pain and offers him the help he needs.

One day, at Satori's request, Cinda tells James of an exhibition of her art that she is planning—a big first step in her career. James is excited and looks forward to the opening. Their meeting with Satori continues as both make positive strides.

On their way back home, James asks, "Am I invited to your opening?"

Cinda chews her bottom lip and does not reply. She seems to be lost in thought.

James tells himself not to feel rejected and not to take it personally. He puts his feelings aside and continues to encourage and share Cinda's good feelings.

Later that night, he prays, "Dear God, please help Cinda learn to be open with me and trust herself. I put my worries in your hands as I now know I cannot accomplish this task for Cinda or without your help. Please expand my horizons and help me to do your work here on earth."

Six weeks pass. James is surprised to see Cinda and Morella on the palace grounds. It is 7:00 a.m., and he is starting on his daily walk with his dogs. Although he meets them unexpectedly, he greets them and offers Cinda congratulations on this, the day of her opening. Then he continues his walk.

A few hours later, at 12:00 noon, coincidentally, James and Cinda meet again. This time, Cinda is with the gardener, who is helping her carry her artwork. James notices the way that her hand lingers on the gardener's arm and feels a stab of jealousy. Morella observes the scene from afar and plans her next attack. James looks away, deciding to ignore his reaction. He gestures towards Cinda's work, compliments her, and wishes her good luck.

He pauses as he wonders why the universe has placed Cinda's event, to which he was not invited, in his face twice that day. James decides to trust that there is a reason and to do his best to let go of any negative thoughts. Deep inside, James feels hurt, but he does not allow himself to take Cinda's actions personally or allow them to ruin the day's work.

Although it takes him longer than usual to attend to affairs of state, James is able to put thoughts of Cinda out of his mind. But at 6:00 p.m., he meets Satori, who is beaming from ear to ear. "Today is Cinda's day. Did she show you her work?"

When James says, "No," Satori asks again, thinking he misheard him. Upon realizing the reality of the situation, Satori lightens the mood with a joke, and James is on his way.

But in the middle of meditation at 9:30 p.m., James cannot stop his thoughts. Sadness overtakes him, and tears well up in his eyes. James's only release is to distance himself from the situation by writing and asking questions to depersonalize the events of the day. James writes out a list of his questions.

(1) How was the truth revealed through the meaning of these events today?

(2) When Cinda chooses not to share a very important and special time of joy, what must I realize?

(3) What does it mean when the universe chooses to speak of Cinda's show to me three times during the same day?

(4) If Cinda chooses to share her work with the gardener and not me, does this mean that they are lovers, or am I jumping to conclusions?

Because he is questioning his own feelings and intentions, he is able to come up with an alternative analysis:

(5) Or do these moments reveal to me that Cinda is distrusting herself?

Not knowing what else to do and still feeling frustrated, James remembers Satori's advice: "First stop the chatter in your head by taking three deep breaths, reflect, and then choose another way to be."

Reflecting, he thinks, *What are my choices? Do I give up or talk about it? I don't want to prejudge without knowing the truth. Since our relationship has grown deeper during our meetings with Satori, and we are communicating, today shows me that there is still work for us to do. I see that our old patterns may be re-emerging.*

James remembers Satori's words: "Choose not to be a vessel of anger. Be optimistic and positive. Beyond pleasure or pain, there is ecstasy. Be empty of thoughts so the clear light of ecstasy can fill you. Do not choose to carry your anger within, or you will become a vessel of anger and continue to hurt yourself. Beyond the mind is the greater self and the perfect light of enlightenment. Be still, be open, give up your individuality; the answers will come."

Upon further reflection, James realizes that the universe knocked three times today with witnesses seeing all: Cinda and Morella at 7:00 a.m., Cinda and the gardener at 12:00 noon, and Satori at 6:00 p.m. James begins to see the situation more clearly through these events. He realizes that he is sensitive to events that are actually happening and what they are trying to show him.

> Your life is like an onion with many layers. Each layer, when understood, can bring you to a deeper awareness.

Later, James asks Satori, "When the universe talks, and the rejecting person does not see it, what do you do?"

Satori nods with understanding. "Nothing. It will do no good to try to make Cinda's journey easier. You sound like you have anger in your voice. Do you want to talk about it?"

James's words gush out; he's relieved to share them with someone else. "I'm angry at Cinda and haven't been able to let it go. I've been trying to see my role in this situation, but I can't."

"When you have anger, Cinda does not hear it, and often she changes the subject by making what happened to be about you—not her. I suggest that by processing your feelings first, you will be able to speak to Cinda from your inner power."

James frowns. "How?"

"My son, understand this situation may be a part of Cinda's journey, not yours. Your journey is to start expressing your feelings appropriately and accurately and to stop running away from them. How will she learn not to blame when you continue to spell her inconsiderateness out to her?"

"Ah," says James while nodding.

Later, James, feeling low in spirits and not knowing what else to do, remembers Satori's advice: "You get what you focus on. Trust yourself."

He decides that he will not allow himself to feel low because of Cinda's seeming disregard for his feelings. He is quite clear that the distrust Cinda is showing is not about him and that she is still unaware of how her actions hurt others.

"Even though I saw her with the gardener today, I trust myself to know deep in my heart that Cinda's love is for me only. When she peels away this layer of her life, she will realize."

James remembers Satori saying, "Your life is like an onion with many layers. Each layer, when understood, can bring you to a deeper awareness."

Questions:
Have you tried using the practice of meditation
to relieve your worries and clear your thoughts?

27

Cinda Has a Moment of Truth

$\mathcal{C}$rowds of people attend Cinda's exhibition, and from the approving looks on their faces, Cinda guesses they are impressed with her work. She takes a moment for herself and stands on the fringes of the crowd, smiling a smile so big her cheek muscles begin to ache. She is finally receiving accolades for the art she has so diligently worked to bring to the public during the past year. She is proud of her success and optimistic about her future in the art world.

Mingled in with the whispers of praise for Cinda's art are the whispers of gossip, speculation on why Prince James is not in attendance. Not escaping the rumor mill is the fact that Morella is present. Cinda had mixed feelings about inviting Morella. She had not forgotten James's remarks about Morella flirting with him. An uneasy feeling about her friend's real motives has settled in her stomach, but in an effort to preserve a relationship in which she has invested so much of herself, Cinda dismisses James's warnings. After all, she considers her flirtations with the gardener to be completely innocent, and believes, against reason, that Morella's are as well.

Cinda's show is successful beyond her boldest expectations. Although elated, she feels a pang of regret and wonders if she should have invited her husband. She purses her lips as she determines that she made the right decision. After all, this is part of her personal journey, and if James were there, she'd be preoccupied with his thoughts and actions. As the final curtain is about to fall, Cinda ignores the crowd, frantically looking for Morella to share the moment with her. However, she is nowhere to be found.

As Cinda enters a hidden room beyond the stage, she hears two very familiar voices: Morella's and the gardener's. She moves closer so as not to miss a word. She hears Morella giggle. "Today is the day when James will have no more of Cinda's nonsense. Soon, he will be mine!"

The gardener replies, "Your plan is succeeding just as you said, Morella. I can't imagine the prince staying after being left out of the most important event of Princess Cinda's career. How did you achieve this?"

Morella laughs. "Cinda does whatever I tell her. I'm the only person she has ever trusted. Now, we just need to start a whisper of a romance between you and Cinda. We'll see that she is caught in compromising circumstances. It will be the end for her, and I will be at James's side to comfort and give him the love he so desperately needs."

"Why do you hate her so much, Morella?"

"She has everything I deserve. It's unfair, but I will set it right ... soon."

"I don't know. This is dangerous. What if the prince finds out?"

"He will never find out. Only you and I know, and you have been paid well for your silence." Morella raises her eyebrows as she pauses, driving the point home. "Now, I must go find Cinda before she becomes suspicious."

Cinda stands frozen to the spot, tears and silent sobs wrenching her body. She hears the crowd in the distance applauding; they are awaiting her appearance. The moment of truth is here. As she faces the guests, a feeling of emptiness replaces the joy that she had felt at the beginning of the evening.

That night, James approaches Cinda to ask about the opening. She seems upset with him, but before the words are out of his mouth, Cinda says, "Please, I can't talk to you now. I will explain everything, but for now, I need to think."

James, wanting to talk, ignores her request for solitude. "I feel that you are still mistrusting and putting all of your blame on me. Is that why you didn't share the opening with me?"

Cinda doesn't want to get into a discussion; she just wants to cry and sleep. She says, "I hear anger in your voice. I don't want to talk to you while you are angry."

James knows now that Cinda does not realize that she fears his anger just as she did her mother's. She is still afraid. James is no longer afraid; he can wait. He calmly replies, "Okay, we will talk again," and does not press her.

Cinda is surprised and relieved. She realizes that she has been afraid of James's anger, but now she feels reassured by his calm behavior. She crawls into bed, crying herself to sleep to escape her pain. In despair, she plans to meet Satori alone before their meeting with James.

James, somehow sensing the princess's distress, cannot sleep either. Cinda, after an hour of tossing and turning, sits up and rubs her eyes. She walks down the long corridor and knocks on James's door. "Are you asleep?"

She is surprised to hear James answer, "No. What's wrong?"

Cinda says hesitantly, "If you don't mind, I would like to visit for a few minutes."

James sees that her fear of him has subsided. Before Cinda can utter a word, James says, "Cinda, my dear, I do want you to be happy and to help you find what is best for you. I wanted to ask you a question before. I was upset that you didn't invite me to your opening. But when I saw you afterwards, you were upset. And yes, I did make that about me, and this prevented you from seeking comfort from me. I can now see that your emotions are not always about me and that by jumping to conclusions, I may have prevented us from communicating."

Cinda looks up at him, and James can now see the streaks of tears on her face as she says, "Thank you for understanding me. I do still love you, James. There are many feelings inside of me right now that run very deep. I need to explore and understand them, and then I'll be ready to tell you about them."

James is relieved. Another storm has passed. He knows that trusting himself gave him the strength to carry on and not back down. His awareness also allowed Cinda the space and acceptance to approach him and express her feelings. James still has many questions, but for now, he will enjoy the moment and the enormous strides they have made.

Questions:

How does the value of trusting yourself expand your life?

How does being honest about your emotions improve your integrity and commitment?

28

A Deceitful Court Plots James's Downfall

$\mathcal{U}$pon awakening the next morning, James is still troubled by the events of the day before, but he puts them aside in order to prepare to meet with King John. He is anticipating a wicked backlash from the men in his court, those he will be replacing after his coronation. Both James and the king have heard rumors about the cabinet plotting behind their backs to discredit young James in order to prevent him from succeeding to the throne. They are eagerly waiting for the moment when James falls from power and is disgraced in his father's eyes. Their plan is to step in and resume the power they are about to lose.

Meanwhile, preparations are being made for another ball. This time, the kingdom will celebrate the coronation of the young King James and the crowning of Queen Cinda. The entire country is looking forward to this day with great anticipation.

Unlike before, King John now keeps a watchful eye on the comings and goings of his inner circle and court. He plans to bring the scoundrels to justice. King John tells Queen Elayna, "In due time, all will right itself. For now, I don't want to give these men any opportunity to bring my son down. Our plans to dispose of their positions will begin after James secretly chooses his new cabinet. Yes, justice will be served, but it will have to wait until after James's coronation."

James's respect for his father continues to grow. His father has recently shown far more intelligence and good sense than James had ever given him credit for. James knows that as king he will seek his father's advice and counsel. He has much to learn, and now, he feels confident in his role. James continues to prepare to assume the reins of power, all the while, in the back of his mind, he is concerned about the situation with Cinda.

Questions:
What positive behaviors did your parents model for you?

29

Cinda's Worst Fears Come True

$\mathcal{T}$hrough a haze of pain and anger, Cinda stumbles along the path to her meeting with Satori. When she finally arrives, she pours out the entire story before the sage can even offer a greeting.

Satori can hardly understand Cinda's words through her sobbing. She asks, "Why have I put my trust in Morella rather than James? He has always loved and cared for me. How can I have been so stupid?"

"My child, your work has been peeling off the layers of mistrust that are ingrained within you. Unaware of the goodness that resides within, your pattern is to gravitate towards people like those in your past. The fear and misgivings you receive from these relationships are what you were used to all of your early life. It is natural

> Your pattern is to gravitate towards people like those in your past.

that you chose Morella at a young age. Although she behaves differently, she is so like your mother—and all you ever knew."

Cinda takes in Satori's words without objecting as she might have done in the past. Satori continues. "What incredible fortitude you must have had in choosing James. My child, your heart knew what was right for you while your head was still living within the patterns you learned as a child."

Cinda chokes back a sob and says, "James really is a miracle, and just as I was told by my mother, I do not deserve him."

Satori shakes his head slowly. "My child, seeing James in only positives does not allow you to accept his whole being. James has flaws just like everyone else. To not recognize them will only cause you to feel inferior in his presence and will create a fear inside of you of disappointing him. This fear comes from the same fear of disappointing your father. James also has this fear inside of him.

"It is your unconscious mind that can get confused, feeling both bad and good. Because you feel undeserving, you cannot allow James's love in. It is you who causes your worst fears to happen and only you who can make a different choice."

Cinda cries, "Satori, what can I do? James will never understand. He gets so defensive when I try to express myself."

"How do you know that, my child? Is your mind still living by the reactions your mother would have had towards you?"

Cinda's mind still reels with confusion, so she chooses to listen to her heart instead. "How can I ever make up for all of my behavior to James?"

"My child, while there are no guarantees, I believe bearing the truth is the way to proceed—no matter what the consequences. Being truthful is the tonic that will heal your life, even if it is painful in the beginning."

Cinda's hears her own voice tremble. "Satori, I am so frightened. From the way I have been raised, my only escape has been through pretending. I deny my feelings and pretend everything is okay."

"Now do you see why you followed Morella's advice over James'?" Satori asks. "You assumed James would do just as you have done so many times. It was indeed familiar to you and gave you a false sense of safety, seeing James as you saw yourself."

"Yes, being absolutely truthful is new ground for me. I'm scared of the consequences."

Satori gives her a look of understanding. Then he speaks softly and slowly, "Although it is easier to lie in the beginning, the web we create for ourselves becomes so tangled that we find little escape in it. Most importantly, our lies rob us of true inner peace and happiness."

Cinda absorbs each word as if she were a dry plant needing the nourishment of water to live.

When Cinda returns home meditation helps her listen to her heart and go deep within. She trusts Satori's wisdom. She knows it will be difficult in the beginning but does believe the truth will free her. She is so tired of a life of pretending and covering up her feelings.

No wonder I have been unhappy and overwhelmed so often. I must have the courage to face myself, she thinks determinedly.

Her dream had revealed that without courage and veracity, her father's life failed him. Now she could choose to learn from his example.

"I will wear Daddy on my right-hand shoulder from here forward as he has given me the greatest of gifts: knowing deep within what not to do. And I will choose integrity and honesty!" she vows.

The next evening, Cinda dreams of her father once again. This time, she sees herself telling her father how disappointed she is in him. "Daddy, why did you leave me and not come back for me as you promised? Was I that unimportant?"

Her father answers, "I was a coward, Cinda, and I did not have the courage to speak up to your mother. Instead, I allowed her to call me names and tell me that I would never amount to anything. I should never have listened to her or believed her, but I did. My mistake caused me to lead a life of failure."

Cinda's body shudders. She takes a long moment to think; as she pictures the many fights she has had with James. She finally says, "I also call James names, even when I do not mean to. I realize that at these times, I am treating James the way Mother treated you."

"Yes, my princess, please do not do to yourself what I allowed your mother to do to me. Maybe you can learn from my mistakes. Please do not be like your mother towards James. You are bright and intelligent, and you can accomplish whatever you want to. I made the mistake of thinking that I was not worthwhile and that I would never amount to anything. My thoughts allowed me to feel beaten up by your mother, and I did not have the courage to fight back. My little princess, I know you do have courage and you will do whatever it takes to put your marriage on the right footing."

Cinda wakes up feeling astonished by her dream. She had not realized how she was imitating the negativity of her mother or how weak her father was. Although her father could not teach her by example, his words were powerful, and Cinda plans to remember them. While they came to her in a dream, she feels deeply inside that they are true.

"Truth and courage will guide me, and true acceptance will be my reward. From here forward, I will learn to find the good in the bad, as Satori has told me to do." Cinda now realizes that James is good, and not bad, not what her mother told her about men at all. Cinda decides that maybe her mother was wrong. All she did was see the bad in Cinda's father, and she made it worse by her words.

"Although Daddy did not have the courage to stand up for himself, I do have courage. Daddy is right, because James would not have fallen in love with me unless he saw something special in me," Cinda declares aloud.

Questions:
How do you think the truth will free you?

30

James Searches for Truth

The atmosphere is tense as James and Cinda meet with Satori this evening. James has anxiously awaited this dialogue about the opening. Although Cinda and James are progressing towards communicating authentically, Satori observes that their new pattern appears to be two steps forward, one step backward—but fortunately, not as far back as where they started. The sage knows he must explore with them the process by which progress is maintained, so they do not risk losing their hard-won advances.

Satori watches Woodrow on Cinda's lap. The little dog is kissing her face. Then, he stares deeply into James's eyes, attempting to ease some of the tension.

To James's surprise, as their dialogue begins, his distrust of Cinda gently fades away. Woodrow snuggles between him and Cinda with his head on Cinda's lap and his tiny legs stretching towards James, creating a bridge between them.

Cinda decides to jump right in. "I did not invite you to the opening because I was nervous and worried that I was making a fool of myself. Even though I knew you were hurt, I felt angry that you wanted me to answer to you—as if I were a child."

James pauses, temporarily rendered speechless by the abruptness of Cinda's confession. "Cinda, I believe the universe was speaking to me yesterday. When Satori innocently asked me about the opening, I thought, *What signs should I pay attention to?* It was then that I realized the answer might not be as simple as I first thought. I understood that you were angry and not I. Through self-reflection, I came to realize that there may be a deeper meaning in your actions."

As Cinda processes some of her feelings, she explains, "I am angry, but it is not towards you, James. It is towards myself and my father." She starts crying. "You see, my father left too soon and never saw any of my accomplishments. I was still afraid you were like my father. I was afraid you would criticize my work ... I was afraid of disappointing you."

> **Many times we push what we want the most out of our lives.**

James mirrors and empathizes. "I am not your father. I did not leave you. But, Cinda, when you shut me out, you push me away, and then I push myself away." James sighs before continuing. "I can see how you would be afraid of my reaction. I have reacted in anger so many times before."

Cinda willingly mirrors James.

Satori adds, "Many times we push what we want the most out of our lives. Cinda, why are you still pushing

James away?" There is a long silence in the room. James does not attempt to fill it.

Satori turns to James. "James, how have you pushed Cinda away?"

James leans forward. "I too have fears from my early patterning that keep me from expressing myself and accepting myself fully. I push Cinda away with anger or by leaving and therefore avoiding the problem."

Cinda is relieved to hear James speak so honestly.

James turns to Cinda. He takes her hand in his as he says, "I have loved no one but you. Your honesty and newly acquired ability to grow and learn from your mistakes is a great gift to the children and me. I appreciate it."

Cinda gives James's hand a gentle squeeze. "I promise to live one day at a time and to be honest with you. I will not project the hateful feelings I grew up knowing onto you anymore. However, I ask you to let me know when I do."

"In keeping with my vows to integrity, I promise," her prince responds.

Cinda continues. "I realize that I am worthy and deserving, as Satori has been saying. Thank you for giving us a second chance. It is what we each deserve."

"I also pledge to live one day at a time and wear these lessons on my right shoulder. Each time I feel afraid to tell you my truth, I will touch my shoulder. This will be an anchor to remind me that the habit of speaking daily truth will be the medicine to bring back the magic of the love we once held so dear."

Satori declares, "Forewarned is forearmed."

"Yes," Cinda says contemplatively, "as we express our truth daily, we will be cleaning our minds of negative emotions and feelings. We will work towards complete and whole acceptance of each other. We'll have a much easier life to look forward to."

"'To thine own self be true,'" quotes James. "That will be our sword and shield to rid us of criticism, blame, and shame."

"Congratulations, my children," Satori says smiling, "for not harboring any more resentment and having the courage to start anew."

Questions:

How does living one day at a time and expressing your truth each day help create happiness?

How does living one day at a time prevent the past from reoccurring?

31

Cinda and James Learn to Work Together

Having resolved the issue of the art show, Cinda is eager to continue her progress. She does not want to risk losing what she and James have worked so hard for. With Woodrow at her side, Cinda asks, "How do we change, Satori?"

Having waited so long for this question Satori smiles in relief. "I have found it helpful to replace the child's messages in your old brain with new, more positive ones."

James frowns. "What do you mean?"

"When you look inside, can you see Little Cinda and Little James crying out for love?"

Satori waits for one of them to respond. To his surprise, it is Cinda who speaks first. "Yes, Satori, I feel the sadness within Little Cinda. As a child, she had to attend to her own needs, without any adult guidance."

While James continues to focus on Little James, Satori instructs Cinda, "Give Little Cinda a hug and tell her, 'From now on, I will be your new mommy. I will give you the love your old mommy did not know how to give.' When you give Little Cinda hugs and affirming messages, which are what she needs, you will eventually be able to do the same for Little James and Little James for Cinda. How can you love another, when you do not know how to love yourself?"

Cinda quickly responds, "I did not realize until now that when I feel ignored, I feel like a child once again. It seems like I can not get enough attention to satisfy my needs; I have been starving for so long."

Satori speaks firmly. "Cinda, dear, remember that as the adult part of you learns to nurture Little Cinda, she will not feel abandoned emotionally ever again. I will continue to teach you, the adult, who is always with Little Cinda how to tend to her needs so that she does not feel alone and vulnerable."

Cinda nods her thanks.

"I would like you to hold up your dominant hand and feel how strong it is. Now, place your dominant hand over your non-dominant one. Do you feel the difference?"

Cinda follows Satori's directions. "Yes, my dominant hand is much stronger than my non-dominant hand."

James too is following along with Cinda and Satori.

"Correct. Your non-dominant hand represents Little Cinda, while your dominant hand represents the strong, adult part of you. Now, take a moment and visualize Little Cinda. When you do, repeat after me. 'Little Cinda, I am an adult now—I am your new mother who has come from your future to take care of you. I look forward to answering your questions whenever you feel the need. But please remember to ask when the timing is right and not when

I am preoccupied or busy with other work. For when the timing is right, I promise you, you will be heard. Everything must be done according to divine love and timing.'" Satori pauses and then asks, "Now, Cinda, how do these words feel to you?"

"They make me feel good. But how will I remember them?"

"I am going to tell you again, one sentence at a time. As you hear what I say, I want you to repeat each sentence aloud. Afterwards, you can write it all down so you can nurture Little Cinda before bedtime with these words."

Cinda repeats the words several times until she says, "I have it."

Satori congratulates Cinda on her progress. "That is wonderful, Cinda. Now that these words make sense to you, I want you to condense what you have learned into a few very clear and important sentences."

"Little Cinda," she begins, "I, the adult, am here to take care of your needs. You do not have to take care of mine. You will never be alone again."

"As you say these words to Little Cinda one hundred times, three times a day, you are beginning to nurture yourself from within."

Cinda's eyes widen at the number of times she must say the words each day. Satori interrupts her thoughts, "One hundred times takes less than five minutes, my dear." Cinda is amazed once again that Satori knew what she was thinking. Then she set her jaw, determined to do whatever it takes. "Thank you, Satori. I will do as you say."

James smiles, having enjoyed watching Cinda and Satori work together. As Satori turns his attention to

James, he asks, "James, what can you say to Little James to make him feel secure and safe?"

James's cheeks redden and he squirms in his chair. He looks from Satori to Cinda and back to Satori as they wait for his response. Hesitantly, he begins, "Little James, I am the adult, and I am here to take care of your needs. You do not have to feel responsible for the feelings of others anymore. I will help you learn how to take care of your own needs."

Satori exclaims, "Wonderful, children! The words you have spoken to Little James and Little Cinda are very powerful and will put you on the path to healing your childhood wounds. I am very proud of you both.

"What I would like you to do now is to thank Little James and Little Cinda for sharing their feelings with you and gently place them into your heart where they will be safe and free to receive your care and attention."

There is much for Cinda and James to think about in the evening. As they leave, Satori notices they are holding hands, and Cinda is looking up at James with love in her eyes. At that moment, there is no distance in their body language. They are smiling and happy as they walk off towards the palace.

Questions:

Why is it important for you to tend to the needs of the little child in you?

What does the little child in you need?

32

Cinda Develops Self-Acceptance

*O*ver the next few days, Cinda makes a conscious effort to follow Satori's instructions and help Little Cinda let go of fear and blame and move towards honesty, responsibility, and acceptance. She decides to consult with Satori to ensure that she is indeed doing as he instructed.

"Satori, I finally understand the meaning of my commitment to integrity towards myself. I can see that it will take me some time until I can truly understand myself."

Satori replies, "My child, change takes time and patience. I am delighted to see that you have made the commitment to helping Little Cinda. I do hope James has made the same commitment as well."

Cinda looks at the sage thoughtfully. "What I want to know is how I can help Little Cinda learn that she can trust me."

"Can you imagine Little Cinda inside of you? Ask her, 'Little Cinda, what messages have you been sent as a child?'"

Cinda focuses her thoughts inward and slowly says, "I keep hearing the words, 'You selfish brat. No one can ever love you.'"

"I see these are your child's messages from your old brain." Satori pauses, waiting for Cinda to focus her attention on him. He then speaks slowly and deliberately. "Now, my child, can you see how important it is for you to replace your child's old brain messages with the new ones?"

Cinda responds quickly. "Yes, that makes sense to me. I have never believed—I mean, Little Cinda has never believed 'I am good, I deserve love.' Her thoughts tend to be more negative and self-defeating. How can I change this, Satori?"

"As you give new affirming messages to Little Cinda, she will no longer feel frightened, alone, or unloved. Let us find the most accurate words for you to say aloud one hundred times three times a day. Saying them aloud helps your new brain absorb the messages more deeply and thus make the needed change. It will take five minutes, three times each day for you to feel the truth deep inside for the first time. Let's start with, 'I am good. I deserve love.'"

Cinda obliges and practices saying these words first to herself, then to Little Cinda. When she is finished repeating them one hundred times, she says, "The first fifty times the words felt hollow, but after another fifty, they were gradually beginning to seep inside my heart."

"As you give the little child within you positive messages one hundred times, three times a day with perseverance and commitment, you will begin to feel them inside as truth. Although the practice is alien to you now, over time, it will become a precious part of your life."

"Just out of curiosity, what if I choose not to say these words aloud to myself?" she inquires.

"To begin your work towards creating inner trust, peace, and commitment to yourself, you must understand that you will only accomplish what you focus on," Satori replies.

Cinda hangs her head. "I understand, Satori. It is just that I cannot imagine anyone loving me. Deep down, I do not believe I am worthy."

Satori speaks softly, with love, kindness, and firmness. "Cinda, this message arises again and again in your mind, does it not?"

Cinda nods.

"Can you see why you *must* find a new message with which to replace it? Do the work Little Cinda needs you to do to give her the ability to trust she never had. When you are honest with her, she will be able to begin to feel she deserves to be loved. Only then will you be ready to feel the fullness of James's love and love James in return. When have you last hugged the little child within you?"

Cinda wrinkles her nose. "Never."

"Cinda, my dear ... then do it now."

Cinda hesitates, looks at Satori, sighs, and finally reaches deep inside of herself and gives Little Cinda a hug that brings a rush of sadness, relief, and hope over her.

Satori blinks back tears of his own. "How did Little Cinda feel?"

Cinda smiles shyly and nods, feeling better than she has felt in a very long time.

Questions:

How do you feel when you nourish and comfort the little child in you?

33

James Develops Self-Respect

*S*oon after, James decides to meet with Satori alone, as he too seeks guidance in his personal journey towards self-realization. Over the past week, James has been trying to follow Satori's advice to the best of his abilities and has noticed a change in his perception of himself and also of Cinda. He and Cinda have been interacting more, and the bond between them has strengthened. He is excited about the progress and looks forward to the upcoming trip he and Cinda have planned, in which they will visit the rulers of a nearby kingdom. *We'll have a blast!* He thinks to himself.

Satori opens the meeting by asking James, "What does commitment to integrity towards yourself mean?"

James stumbles a bit, not anticipating the pop quiz. "Well…" Unlike previously, this question is one that forces him to think rather than respond emotionally. "Integrity is about having my own thoughts and heeding my own words."

Satori responds with a quizzical look on his face. "My child, your definition of integrity is more in line with that of defensiveness."

James is perplexed. "Is integrity not about making choices that are consistent with your needs no matter what the circumstance?"

"To behave in such a way would require that you only think of yourself and not how your actions affect others."

James shifts uncomfortably and focuses on the ground in front of him.

"Integrity is at the core of what you and Cinda have been working towards. It is the concept of living by the principles you choose for your life. This includes not only aspects of your own self, but also those of your family and your kingdom. To have integrity is to live with commitment, honesty, acceptance, and responsibility—free of blame and criticism and judgment. It is the path to change the present and put the past in the past. When you follow these principles, in time, you and Cinda will become stronger and rid yourselves of the old patterns."

"Satori, you must have a method that will help us stop ourselves when either of us sees the past repeating itself. What do we do to move into the present? How do we eliminate our feelings of blame towards ourselves and others?"

"There is a method that can help change such patterns. It is simpler than you can imagine. The hardest part is remembering to use it when needed. When you are aware that you have just repeated a pattern, do the following: Stop, breathe deeply five times, reflect upon what is happening, and choose an action that will help. That will put you in the place you choose to be and will help you to respond out of respect rather than anger."

James asks in confusion, "Yes, but when Cinda upsets me and I get angry, how can I let her know that her actions have hurt me?"

"Son, look to your own past, and you will recognize the feelings Cinda triggers in you. It will take thought, but when you see why you respond the way you do, identify who Cinda is reminding you of in the moment. Then stop, take five deep breaths, reflect to yourself (just as you are doing to me), and choose what you will do."

James thinks for a moment before responding. "I know that when Cinda disregards me, my father comes to mind and I become angry. Thank you, Satori. Because I know I am in charge of my behavior and my response to Cinda. I will plan to use your method to change the way I respond. I will also take time to meditate and discover if there is more to the source of my anger."

Satori smiles with great satisfaction with his pupil's progress. "In this way, you will begin each moment anew, rather than build resentments."

"Now I understand," James says. "By stepping away and using your method, I am interrupting my pattern, and therefore, I am changing the way I react in the present and not allowing the bitter past to creep in."

"Yes, James. And by choosing your reactions, you develop more respect and integrity for yourself and for Cinda."

James can see how his past angry outbursts and choice to avoid or leave the situation had only served to continue old patterns. For the first time, he is able to recognize that what he thought were behaviors based in integrity were actually attempts to protect himself from taking responsibility for the situation.

"Satori, because I plan to keep my commitments to myself and Cinda and do what I say I will do, I promise myself and Cinda not to accept anything less than respect for myself and for her. I can see that the blame we project onto each other does not come from the present but from fear and the past. Even if it takes me until the next day to realize I feel wounded, I will still take the steps that you have outlined at that time."

Reinforcing the message, Satori says, "My child, each time you follow through with your commitment to yourself, you are strengthening your integrity. This is where your new, improved relationship will truly begin. Did I tell you the unwritten law of human relationships?"

"No."

Satori proudly states, "A relationship without respect is no relationship at all. Likewise, a relationship without trust is also no relationship. As you obey this law, you will steer your own ship, rather than have it steer you. This is a time of intensity in your relationship.

"One last thought: Remember, do not go to bed angry! Instead, say, 'I am changing the way I react in the present, and I would like to discuss my feelings.'"

James thanks his mentor, and says, "I will relay these new messages to Cinda as soon as I see her." Satori smiles in agreement. Having learned a lot today, James is eager to get back to Cinda and apply this newfound knowledge to his relationship.

Questions:

How does taking the blame out of your life help you develop the habit of learning from your mistakes and correcting them?

Why do you think this habit will help you find happiness and alleviate pain?

At what times, during your weak moments, do you react to your partner the way your parents reacted to each other; or the way you reacted to your parents as a child?

34

James and Cinda Receive Prescriptions for Happiness

*C*inda and James have one more visit with Satori before they leave for their trip, and the sage has something special in store for them.

"Hello, my children. Today is the first day of the rest of your lives. Therefore, it is time to begin to change your brain's early programming."

James looks puzzled. "But that is what we have been working on—changing old patterns."

"You are correct, James, but remember developing awareness takes time and requires constant review. Have you kept your promises to put difficult conversations on hold for a later discussion with me or through a dialogue in order to avoid old patterns of name-calling or walking away?"

"Most of the time," James responds.

Cinda adds, "We have been changing the way we respond to each other. Instead of exploding or walking away when we are about to have an argument, we stop, breathe deeply five times, reflect, and choose. Then we set appointments to talk with each other."

"We are learning that with trust, time, and patience, we are beginning to change our early patterning," James concludes proudly.

Satori smiles. "Your bond will continue to deepen as you discover the underlying issues that instigate your negative behaviors. With your work, a new consciousness will begin to develop.

"Let us review. Why does the child inside of you respond at times in the same old negative way?

Cinda answers, "When either of us incite angry feelings in the other, it is because of our old brain, the child inside of us, is still afraid of the same negative feelings we received from the environment in which we were raised."

"Cinda, are any of the reactions James gives you similar to what your mother did? Or are you not anticipating the same reactions from James?"

Cinda nods. As she answers 'yes' to both questions she is actively listening and absorbing Satori's words.

"It is very difficult to change the early programming which has been with you your entire life. But I do have a suggestion, a prescription if you will, for the both of you. Would you like to hear it?"

"Yes," Cinda and James say simultaneously. They look at each other and smile.

"Your prescription is really quite simple, Cinda. When James criticizes you as you remember your mother doing, begin by being the mother to Little Cinda you did not have. Do not accept James's criticism as true, as that is what you automatically did as a child. Tell Little Cinda,

'James is not your mother.' And understand that James is unaware of his criticism at this moment. Do not take his words personally but set a time to talk to James about how he just made you feel instead."

A lighthearted look appears upon Cinda's face.

Satori continues. "Since you feel acknowledged and heard, you are now giving your new brain a different way to respond."

Cinda nods. "I see. Now I can tell my new brain that James does not mean to hurt me, and when he is critical, it is not personal to me, just his early patterning that he is changing."

"You've got it, my child. You are now helping your new brain to trust—a difficult concept we all must learn."

James has waited patiently with Woodrow on his lap.

Satori gives James his own prescription. "James, yours is very similar to Cinda's as you share the same childhood wounds. Your prescription is to repeat, 'Cinda is not my father. I am not my mother,' and understand that Cinda is not meaning to harm you with her words or behaviors. Then you must set a time to talk with her about how she made you feel."

James nods.

> Since you feel acknowledged and heard, you are now giving your new brain a different way to respond.

"Your new work begins tomorrow morning, the first day of your trip. The trip will give you the time to take on this daily agenda. As you do, you will begin to put the past in the past and live in the present."

The silence in the room is filled with warmth and optimism, and they each hug Satori.

Before leaving, James says, "Satori, I have been so pleased that Woody has been here to comfort me. May I offer him a dog biscuit?"

Satori shakes his head. "No, thank you. One must learn that virtue is its own reward. But Woody will accept a dog biscuit at another time, out of friendship, for he enjoys modeling the unconditional love he gives so automatically. Ah, if only humans had the same ability as Woodrow's species does. We have much to learn from Woody.

"I bid you both a very successful trip. Give my regards to the king and queen."

As they leave, Cinda asks James, "Do you think it is really possible to put the past in the past?"

"Of course! We can accomplish what we focus on. Satori continues to lead us toward our own growth, does he not?"

Cinda smiles at James. "Yes. I guess we will just have to take one day at a time."

James agrees. "Tomorrow will take care of itself. For now, let us have a superb dinner at our favorite restaurant and plan for our trip." He smiles and takes Cinda by the hand.

***

Questions:
What is your prescription for happiness?

35

Love Blossoms Once Again

*A*s their ship approaches their hosts' castle, Cinda again asks James, "How will we ever leave the past behind us?"

James replies with complete confidence, "I remember Satori telling us about the different selves within us; as we unmask them, we begin to release our negative conditioning from our childhood. In this way, we will move on."

Cinda nods in agreement, sighing. "It's quite difficult to travel back to our childhoods to learn from the past."

"It is difficult, but it is a challenge we must accept. It is in the present that we distort the moments. We cannot allow anything to rob us of our magic. When we are able to reveal our fears and insecurities, the natural part of us will express itself without past fears interfering."

Cinda smiles. "I look forward to that day. Do you?"

"Yes, very much." James puts his arms around Cinda as the sunset envelops their yacht. James is once again amazed at how good he feels. He believes that they are finally able to fight for their marriage.

A light appears in James's eyes. He remembers his mother telling him, "I am trying not to allow your father to be so critical of us." Now he can see that trying is not enough—standing up to his father without fearing the consequences is the only way. Either his mother was not strong enough or she did not have integrity towards herself. By not honoring herself, the struggle robbed her of positive feelings for her life.

James wonders, *Have I copied Mother?* He is astonished at his own thoughts. Then aloud to Cinda, he again reaffirms his vow to integrity towards himself: "I will not accept disrespect to you or from you from this day forward. I cannot afford to step backwards. The price is too high to pay for our children, our kingdom, and myself. I vow to stop repeating the behavior of my past."

Cinda is a bit taken aback as this seems to come from out of the blue. But she makes a concerted effort to listen intently. "I know you mean what you say, my love. Thank you for respecting yourself and for supporting and respecting me. I find myself loving you more each day because of it." Cinda, seeing the change in James, makes a sacred promise to herself at that moment that when she returns from her trip, she will do the work needed to confront her mother so that she is indeed rid of the negativity that still resides within her.

During the two-week visit, Cinda and James repeat their respective prescriptions, and the time passes pleasantly. Cinda feels involved in her husband's work and revels in being an important figure in his relationships with others.

James feels grateful to have such solid support from Cinda. He also feels Cinda's pride and admiration and realizes that this aspect of their marriage is finally reawakening. He notices that when Cinda begins to trust herself, it helps her to trust him and that when he views Cinda with love and respect; he too begins to trust her. The affection between them is blossoming once again, and their visit is all too soon finished.

At home, Cinda and James tell Satori of the trip, relating the special moments. They both are confident a new era in their lives has begun. With a broad grin and a hearty handshake, James reaches out towards Satori. "Thank you again for helping me find my internal power."

Satori senses the love in the couple's hearts as he congratulates them on making the difficult journey. "Although I have a white beard and appear to be aged, the years have ripened me. I have been around this world many times. But in all my journeys and work, I have never felt such satisfaction. Thank the gods that I felt you from afar and your aura brought me to you."

Woodrow gleefully wags his tail, this time jumping on Satori's lap—suprising everyone.

Before they leave, James adds his own bit of wisdom. "We must remember this moment and teach our children that perseverance is the key that continually opens the doors to a growing relationship. This above all is the magic that will keep our relationship flowing."

Satori embraces the couple. "I just want you two to know how much gratitude I feel for having been able to assist the future King James and Queen Cinda. I have waited many centuries to witness such perseverance as the two of you have shown me; it holds such great promise. It has been a goal of mine throughout the centuries. Now, I will hold you up as an example to others who come to me seeking the wisdom of a happy, enduring relationship."

Questions:
When you approach your relationship with positive perceptions, what messages become available to you and your partner and your marriage?

36

Prince James Routs His Enemies
and Saves the Kingdom

*T*he short vacation has renewed James's energy. With the knowledge that he has Cinda's love and support, he feels ready to face anything. As it turns out, he will need all his courage and strength to deal with his enemies at court.

James learns from the king that the courtiers are planning a meeting in which they will offer what they believe is incontrovertible proof that James has misused the kingdom's funds. James is actually relieved that the day has come when he will finally have his chance to set matters straight and to resolve this issue once and for all.

The court convenes two days later. After the deceitful courtiers present their evidence of funds not accounted for and strut back to their seats, sure of James's downfall, the young prince stands and addresses the king and his court. "I appreciate your diligence, men. I am prepared to show receipts for all the money that has been spent without your knowledge. You see, in my haste to prepare for my trip, I had to immediately authorize emergency funds to feed the southern part of Lavonia that you know was hit with disastrous floods once again on the very day I was leaving.

"The people have had a difficult time sustaining themselves, and this latest flood put them over the edge. Food, shelter, and medical supplies had to be brought in, in order to help our southern province. I continued receiving word of the work being done while on my trip. Fortunately, it has saved many lives. We will have to administer more funds in the near future. I had planned to update the entire court on what was needed when I returned."

King John is beaming with pride once again as he witnesses his son's confidence and fortitude. The men, aware that they took no actions to help the southern province when James left for his trip, scramble to offer suggestions for added help. They realize their dastardly plot has failed. James adds, "I plan to modernize our farms and have been studying a new levy system to prevent future flooding. In the future, we will meet to discuss my ideas to bring the budget into balance and put aside funds for the needed improvements." The court is stunned.

As plans for the coronation continue, James and his father are aware they will have to remain vigilant against whatever schemes their enemies will try next, but, for now, the court has been quieted and a time of celebration is at hand.

Cinda also wishes to confront her hidden enemy, her false friend, Morella. However, the treacherous woman fled when she realized that her true nature had been discovered. She feared Cinda's wrath, as she knew well what she would have done to such an enemy in her place. However, Cinda, having learned to accept and trust herself, does not need revenge against Morella. In addition to a great pity for the unhappy creature, Cinda feels a small bit of gratitude. Morella's schemes and plans inadvertently pushed the princess along the path to her current happiness.

Questions:
What will help you to develop confidence in yourself?

37

James and Cinda Continue to Grow

As Cinda now sees hope, she is actively using her prescription for happiness and continues to help to heal the hurt in Little Cinda. She has also received assistance from Satori to do the necessary work of confronting her mother, keeping a promise she made to herself on their trip. She feels proud that she is not ignoring Little Cinda and is doing the work she knows is best for Little Cinda's growth.

James too has been doing his part. He has developed insight into his own behavior, has not reacted angrily towards Cinda, and has helped to heal the hurt in Little James. Now, they both enthusiastically await each meeting with Satori and have many questions to ask.

As soon as they arrive for their meeting this day, Cinda bursts out with a statement. "Satori, I have been pondering the meaning of perception and how perception can play a role in our marriage."

Satori is delighted at the new level of insight that is emerging in the couple. "My children, you are becoming conscious and are beginning to scratch the surface of understanding each other.

"As you unravel your deepest childhood wounds, you begin to realize why you react as you do to each other. Cinda, one of your deepest wounds from childhood obviously comes from being criticized and not listened to by your mother. Your wound, similar to Cinda's, James, comes from the criticism and disrespect you received from your father. Once again, you are noticing that you handle your wounds in opposite ways. As we have said before, that is the unconscious attraction you originally had towards one another."

> As you unravel your deepest childhood wounds, you begin to realize why you react as you do to each other.

James shakes his head and breaks in. "Satori, it is hard to believe that although at first I was attracted to Cinda's positive traits, I unconsciously felt comfortable with her underlying negativity and criticism."

"Yes, my son, although the wounds for each couple are different, the process of attraction and the developmental stages in marriage are similar. Your old way, James, when you were criticized, was to run away as you did when a child. While you, Cinda, when you were criticized, you attacked in your defense as you learned

to do as a child. The same wound, criticism, is handled in opposite ways. As each of you heals your own
wounds, you will be healing your partner's wounds in
the process."

James frowns, not quite understanding fully. "How
am I healing Cinda's wounds when I am not even partially
healed myself?"

Cinda answers before Satori has a chance to speak.
"Why, James, you have taught me that you no longer tolerate my criticism. And I have learned that when I criticize
you, it causes you to lose love for me. I am being forced
to heal because I want to have you in my life and to rid
myself of my mother's nastiness."

Satori smiles at Cinda's eloquent summary and insight.
"Cinda, your response would not have been possible many
weeks ago."

James nods. "I feel the same way, Cinda. It seems
that I am rarely upset for the reason I think. It is usually all about me. As my business as prince is constantly
changing, I am reacting to a changing environment.
That is the way kingdoms work. But with the added pres-
sure of feeling responsible for your feelings, it became
overwhelming.

"My underlying fear of not being good enough eroded
my confidence. It is amazing how I allowed that fear to
keep me off balance and unhappy. In reality, I rarely
received criticism, except from you. While my people look
to me for leadership, I have been using my fear to cause
my own suffering." James suddenly begins laughing.

Satori's shaggy eyebrows go up in surprise. "What is so funny, my son?"

James says, "I said it without thinking—but it's true. I use my fear to suffer."

"People who change and evolve are the ones who keep working on themselves. I used to be like you, too, James, when I lacked trust in myself."

"You?"

"Yes, while I used to second-guess my thoughts, I now rely on my thoughts to avoid the negativity of others. As a result, I am enjoying every day."

"Is that the secret of life?" James asks.

"My son, life's enjoyment stems from living in the present. I find it challenging and pleasurable to react from inner trust rather than past misperceptions."

James looks directly at Cinda. "That is the part of you I have been reacting to, my love. I have allowed your distrust of me to cause me to doubt myself."

Cinda returns his look. "And I am happier when I no longer allow your negative energy to cause me to react defensively—or should I say, what I perceive as negative energy." She laughs, and James and Satori join her.

Satori adds, "I have learned to feel empowered by the saying, 'What you think of me is none of my business.' That way, I am more concerned with my thoughts, rather than what others think of me. It is very helpful for feeling the integrity within myself; and eliminates any doubts and insecurities I may have. After all, I can only do my very best. I put the rest in God's hands.

Questions:

How does understanding your childhood wounds help you realize why you react as you do to your partner?

What can you do to change that reaction?

38

Cinda and James Take Responsibility for Their Own Healing

*A*t their next meeting, Cinda decides to bring up a subject that has been bothering her. "James, you have shown me trust by not asking, but I want to tell you that I did not respond to you after the show because I knew I had a lot of processing to do with Satori. I am sorry that I was inconsiderate of your feelings and that I caused you so much turmoil."

"Thank you, Cinda. I appreciate your candidness."

"By persevering and waiting, you gave Cinda the space she needed to come to terms with her feelings which have been in the way of her relationship with you," Satori explains, making sure James understands the full meaning of Cinda's statement.

James nods, adding, "I, too, have been rewarded by learning how to wait and trust."

As they each hug, Woodrow comes bouncing into the room exactly on cue to give them goodbye kisses. James and Cinda are quite content as Satori reviews what they have already learned. "My children, as you know that your wounds are similar but handled in different ways, can you see why you have found yourselves trapped in a continuous cycle of negativity?"

Cinda answers first. "Is this because our reactions have come from our childhood fears rather than our higher selves?"

> Then is it true that by becoming aware of my childhood wounds, and how they are triggered in me, I am breaking old patterns of negative behavior, and in time, I will be able to give up suffering?

"Yes, you are quite right, my child. Your higher selves do not want you to suffer, but to trust instead."

James adds, "Then is it true that by becoming aware of my childhood wounds, and how they are triggered in me, I am breaking old patterns of negative behavior, and in time, I will be able to give up suffering?"

"Exactly, my son. When you continue questioning why you respond as you do, you become conscious of your wounds as they are happening. For example, James, when you feel Cinda is talking to you in a deprecating tone of voice, you now recognize the source of your frustration—in this case, your father. By raising Cinda's consciousness of how she is triggering these feelings in you, through the mirroring process, you have several options open rather than just walking away and not facing the situation."

Cinda jumps in, as she is eager to convey the depth of her change and growth. "James, because I have learned to trust myself, and in turn you, I am beginning to become the mother I wish I had. By being one with Little Cinda, I show her she can trust me and that I am always here for her. It works. It really does! Thank you, James, for being you. And thank you, Satori, for your wisdom and inner strength."

"It is my pleasure to see that my words have taken root, my child. Also, when you give Little Cinda the love your mother failed to give her, you become less fearful and more self-assured."

Cinda smiles in surprise. "It is true! I no longer require James to provide for my every need. I am doing that quite well myself these days. Now I am aware that our marriage was unhealthy when I expected James to give me the love my mother never gave me."

"Yes," says Satori, nodding in understanding, "most people think that when they fall in love, their partner will make them happy forever after. It cannot be so, and that is why romantic love lasts but only a few moments in time. It is you who must learn to nurture the child inside of you and to be at one with yourself. It is you who must take on the role of being loving and all providing to the child inside of you. Then inner peace, self-confidence, and happiness shall be your reward. That is how you heal your childhood wounds. No one can do that for you; you must be the one."

Questions:
How does not taking another's words
personally free you to enjoy the moments?

39

The Journey Continues

*H*aving congratulated the couple on their progress, Satori's face becomes serious once again. He says, "I have one last lesson for both of you to learn. Are you each willing to begin the process of taking total responsibility for what you say and do? My spiritual intuitiveness tells me that you two have the fortitude to achieve this most difficult of tasks—to do whatever it takes to keep your sacred promise."

James responds immediately. "Satori, I am here today for no other reason. I promise I shall continue to do whatever it takes for the sake of my marriage, my children, and my kingdom."

He takes Cinda's hand and looks deeply into her eyes. "Cinda, my dear, I love you with all of my heart even though our marriage has been on tenuous grounds. I hope you are also willing to do what it takes for our lives and the lives of our children. I promise from the bottom of my heart you will never regret it. We are truly blessed to have found a man like Satori who will help us."

Cinda is deeply touched by her husband's sincerity. The lively girl within her is now determined to do the job. Cinda rises to the occasion, takes the challenge, and says, "All right, James, I am with you. If you can do it, so can I … so can we."

"You both must promise not to blame the other for what bothers you. Choose to eliminate blame, shame, and criticism from your lives forever, and the process of bringing back romance will begin. When you master this concept, the love that returns to you will be stronger and deeper than it was when you were in the romantic phase of marriage.

"Think of this as an ancient jousting tournament. Your enemies are your old negative thought patterns. Are you both still on the playing field?" When they respond affirmatively, Satori says, "Very well, put on your helmets, and let the games begin. Look at the possibility of understanding that what you do not like about the other is what you dislike in yourself."

James asks, "Do you actually mean that what I do not accept in Cinda is what I dislike in myself?"

"Yes, my son. Ask yourself what makes you most uncomfortable with Cinda."

James squirms in his seat and adjusts the top button of his shirt. "I am very uncomfortable when Cinda's emotions come out of nowhere and overwhelm me."

"My son, what do you do with your emotions?"

"I work very hard to keep myself calm, no matter what happens."

"Please take a moment, James, to say, 'When Cinda goes into a rage, it reminds me of when I was a child and ...'"

James's face reddens. He continues to squirm. "It reminds me of my father's rages. They were embarrassing. But I had no other choice than to hold my feelings inside. I never wanted to behave like Father. Perhaps you are right, Satori. I can see why I ran away."

Cinda is amazed at her own reactions. Without thinking, she blurts, "James, when you spoke to me with a firm and sincere tone and did not yell or scream, it was then that I began working very differently with Satori. Setting your boundaries very firmly helped me to change."

"Is that all, my child?" prompts the wise man.

She says confidently, "No, my real awakening came when I realized that I would truly lose you, if I did not change."

James quietly remembers the saying Satori had told him so often, 'When you change the way you respond to the other, they do the thing they are doing MORE. When it no longer works, they change the way they respond or react to you.' James knew this to be true, as he thought, *When I stopped allowing myself to respond to Cinda's blame, shame, criticism and complaints about all I did, she began the process of change by asking for Satori's help. I took the risk that she loved me enough to work on herself. But if she did not, I could not have stayed in such an unhealthy relationship.*

James's thoughts go back to Satori as he hears, "You become closer each day as you learn more about yourselves. Although you began at opposite ends of the field, your new understanding, knowledge of yourselves, and acquired ability to express your feelings are bringing you the love you desire. Cinda, what can you not tolerate in James?"

"Emotions were certainly expressed in my family, and although a bit extreme at times, I came to rely upon them as barometers to guide me."

Having not received a direct answer to his question, Satori asks again, "And what do you dislike most about James?"

"His tendency to either avoid confrontation or explode in confrontation. James, when you express your feelings and anger to me through dialogue, I trust you at that moment because I know exactly what you are feeling."

James is surprised. "I guess I understand. When I avoided you, or exploded, it created a different fear in me that you would never speak to me again. As a child I was often told that expressing my feelings were selfish actions." James pauses as he reflects on the past. "I guess I copied mother because I remember that is exactly what Mother did to Father."

After another pause, James continues, "Now I can see that the feelings I feared to express caused me to dislike Cinda's ability to express whatever she felt, no matter how painful it was for me."

Cinda also admits, "I realize that the more I understand and accept myself, the more I can love and accept James."

Satori's face lights up with great satisfaction. He tells the couple, "This is the match that will keep the fire of

love burning. As Thomas Byron wrote in *Dhammapada,
The Sayings of the Buddha*:

> You are the source
> Of all purity and all impurity.
> No one purifies another.
> Never neglect your work for another's,
> However great his need.
> Your work is to discover your work.
> And then with all your heart,
> To give yourself to it.

James and Cinda smile, each a little embarrassed, because, of course, this speaks to the very core of their worst arguments.

James says after much thought, "Satori, I believe that I am totally responsible for what I say and do, especially knowing that when anger arises, it is coming from my feelings about myself. I intend to keep this concept at the forefront of my mind."

Cinda also vows to continue the journey. "I will do the same. It amazes me that in the past, we thought we could heal our problems by ourselves. Now I realize that we tried to do the most difficult of all tasks alone."

James interrupts. "It is true. When I want to learn a new sport, I call in a coach. But when I had to change my life, I tried to do it myself. It does not make sense, does it? Why did I feel I had to be an expert in something I knew so little about?"

As they each remember how their parents were, they laugh, but neither openly criticizes the other, as they would have in the past.

Questions:

When do you observe your own behavior and listen to how you respond to others?

When have you realized that what you dislike in your partner is found within yourself? How have you tried to solve the enigma?

How does eliminating blame, shame, and criticism from your life help to deepen your love?

40

Cinda Learns the Power of Forgiveness

The night of the coronation finally arrives. The grand celebration is all that it is meant to be. King James skillfully guides the new queen around the grand ballroom. Amidst magnificent surroundings and beautiful music, James and Cinda dance in synchronicity with each other. All eyes follow their every step as the crowd stares in enchantment at the charming couple. Both the dignitaries and commoners enjoy each and every moment, honored to be attending this momentous occasion.

An unexpected guest is also in attendance. The man dressed in a long black cloak and tall hat is present as at the last ball, once again trying to remain hidden in the dark shadows of the ballroom.

James again catches sight of the man eyeing him very suspiciously.

A few moments later, the man in black approaches James. In a barely audible voice, staring down at the magnificent tiles on the ballroom floor, he mumbles, "I, your highness, am Cinda's father. Would you allow me to speak to her?"

James is flabbergasted but willingly brings him over to meet Cinda. When Cinda's father sees his little princess, now Queen, he bows at her feet with tears clouding his eyes. "My daughter, your highness, can you ever forgive me for leaving you?"

Cinda's mind goes blank. She finds she cannot even look into her father's eyes. The room around her feels as if it is spinning. She cannot believe what is happening in this moment. Her eyes too are filled with tears.

Her father speaks again. "I have regretted my actions every day of my life since I left you. If only I had the courage to face your mother and not allow her to treat me so abusively. Running away was all I was capable of doing then. But I married another woman—far worse than your mother—whom I allowed to abuse me daily, just as I did in my first marriage. Can you forgive me, my child? I swallowed a bitter pill when I left you."

Cinda, in astonishment, recalls her recent dream. She credits her meditation with helping her find the truth. Then she gathers her senses and says, with forgiveness in her heart, "We each learn our lessons in different ways. I'm grateful for all that life taught me and for having learned from adversity."

Cinda's father trembles as the tears continue running down his face. Cinda knows deeply within that her father's actions had caused him to suffer greatly and robbed him of all happiness. "Father, I have waited all my life for this moment." She embraces her father for the first time in a very long time. She knows that if he had not abandoned her, she may never have learned to care for herself. Then, summoning all of her courage, Cinda bravely tells her father, "I have learned what not to do from you, Father, and the example of how you chose to live your life will always serve to remind me to continue to work consciously on improving myself as a wife and parent, for it's my desire to never give up on my children, or myself. Hopefully, James and I will live happily ever after by never neglecting the work we are doing in understanding, acknowledging, and accepting each other, and ourselves. I am grateful for these lessons I have learned as a result of your behavior, Father."

With great relief in his voice, Cinda's father replies, "I gratefully accept your candor; it is what I have brought upon myself. My greatest wish is that we can begin again."

James steps in, knowing Cinda is at a loss as to what else to do. He brings Cinda to his side. "Let us leave the past in the past and profit, instead, from the lessons we have learned."

Cinda regains her composure. "Father, remembering your words that I was meant to be a princess gave me the perseverance to find my prince. Please allow us to follow King James; he is right in saying that we cannot allow the past to rob us of the joy we are experiencing in the present."

Cinda's father is filled with gratitude as he did not ever believe that his daughter would forgive him for his actions or understand his reasons for staying away so long. It had taken all of the courage that he wished he had used in his life to come to the coronation and speak to his daughter. He profited alone from this act.

Cinda has finally been afforded the real-life opportunity to heal the hurt her father caused her as a child. "Forgiveness," she says to him, "is the most precious gift one human can give another. I do forgive you, Father, for I can see clearly that there is good in the bad that happens to us."

Cinda remembered what Satori had taught her, "Forgiveness does not mean, 'What you did is okay to me'. It simply means, 'I am no longer willing to carry around pain in response to your actions.' When we hold unforgiveness in our hearts, we only punish ourselves after all."*

Questions:
How would forgiveness of another heal and simplify your life?

---

*Healing With The Angels, Doreen Virtue, Ph.D.

41

Cinda and James Find a New Kind of Happily Ever After

$\mathcal{S}$everal weeks after the coronation, King James and Queen Cinda are spending their days on the palace grounds playing games with the children, attending sporting events together, and just simply enjoying each other's company. During the difficult times when there is even a hint of Cinda's mistrust, James sits down with her as soon as possible and talks of his intuition and feelings until they are on a solid footing again. Likewise, Cinda has become very skilled at reflecting James's outbursts to him and encouraging a dialogue instead. As both James and Cinda are becoming more aware of each other's feelings, their happiness together grows richer and deeper. There are days when their talks last for hours, as they did in the beginning. Cinda and James each plan to continue working separately with Satori to resolve their issues with their parents, a task that will put any leftover anger and resentment in the past. It is indeed the foundation of a new intimacy they are creating with each other. Satori remains in their lives, although they do not meet as often.

One day, Cinda and James decide to invite Satori for a celebration.

As they are sitting in the gardens surrounded by natural beauty, Cinda says, "Satori, you will always be a part of our life. Thank you."

Satori smiles. "My children, I will continue to assist you in stepping out of your own way and taking time to meditate and think about what happened before you respond to each other the way your parents would have responded. For this is the key to creating relationship magic."

James brings forth a bottle of champagne and three glasses. "I propose a toast to achieving our goals, Satori, and then soon, quite soon, Cinda and I will need your guidance to pass your wisdom and knowledge on to the people of our kingdom!"

"To a bright future and good health to all," Satori toasts, and the three of them drink a toast to the future.

Woodrow is as usual ever so loyal, bounds up and barks with happiness.

Satori beams, knowing he is where the gods have placed him and is indeed fulfilling his purpose. "Peace for the world begins with just two people," he muses quietly.

Cinda proposes an additional toast, "To a new chapter for humankind."

James adds, "Yes, Cinda, and to happily ever after."

The End

Steps to Creating Your Own Relationship Magic

*T*his section is intended to help you get started creating your own relationship magic. In a journal, write the date, time, and the step you are working on. Do not judge yourself or your writing; one sentence is as important as a paragraph as you master these concepts. Work on these steps daily until the thoughts become a part of you. Write notes about how focusing on the one thought helped you begin to change your way of thinking about your relationship. Proceed to the next thought when you are ready. Writing is a way for you to track your progress. Move on to your next step only when you feel confident you have achieved the previous one.

Remember, Satori's goal is to help you acquire the fortitude to tend your own garden and to help you develop the habit of weeding by making it a daily ritual. Knowing you have to nourish yourself before you can nourish anyone else, this is a way of doing it. My advice remains: "One thing at a time and that done well. Rome was not built in a day."

Relationship magic awaits you. Read this section thoroughly before you begin to focus on your first step.

It is more important that you work through each step completely rather than quickly.

Relationship magic steps:

Each day, take ten minutes to relax and breathe deeply five times.

Start by imagining the prince or princess in you for a few minutes.

Then actually feel that you are that person.

Most importantly, believe that you too will manifest your dreams, one day at a time.

Exercise:

Start a new practice. Develop a few words that reflect your new mindset to be repeated for five minutes, three times a day until you change the patterning in your old brain. Over time, you will acquire new perceptions—as your new brain learns to react in a positive manner. When you give your brain new words to say, they will replace the outdated, negative messages that have been running your life.

Five minutes, three times a day, would that not be worthwhile to change your thought patterns and bring you into a peaceful way of being?

You are now giving your new brain a different way to respond. You are now on your way to relationship magic.

Relationship Magic Questions

$\mathcal{T}$he questions from the text are repeated for you here below. Answer the following questions, one at a time. Answer them completely and honestly. These questions will help you see how much you have learned from Cinda and James's story.

As the answers reveal themselves, you will already be finding a clue to why you react strongly to each other in certain instances. After you have answered these questions, you will have a better understanding of the truths about yourself and your relationship.

Questions:

When did disillusionment mar your relationship dreams? What did you do about it?

What are the positive and negative traits of your parents?

Which traits do you find in your partner?

Do you feel responsible for your partner's happiness?

What negative beliefs do you have about your partner's personality and behaviors?

Do you remember the way you acted and reacted towards your partner during the romantic phase of your marriage?

In what ways did you treat him/her then that you are forgetting to do now?

What happened to you as a child that damaged your ability to trust?

How do you react to blame or criticism from your partner?

How did you feel when you were ignored or not listened to when you were a child?

How do you think it affects how you react to your partner today?

What were you taught about expressing yourself as a child?

Did you have to hide your true feelings in order to get your needs met?

What do you remember about the way your parents treated you?

What are your beliefs about sharing wisdom with others?

What are your beliefs in a higher power?

Do you intend to find a mentor whom you can trust for guidance and wisdom?

What are some fears that you have not expressed?

What would give you the courage to express concern to the parent you have had the hardest time dealing with?

What incident in your childhood taught you that you could not provide happiness for another?

Have you noticed that persistently changing the way you react to the other person causes him or her to change the way he or she reacts to you?

What aspect of Satori's personality helps Cinda to feel loved and secure?

What aspects of your partner's personality help you feel loved and secure?

What encourages you to see that mirroring what the other person says helps you to truly understand what he means?

What excuse do you use to avoid taking responsibility?

How does committing to integrity to yourself help you to feel safe in expressing your feelings?

How can you learn to practice more assertive communication, rather than aggressive or passive communication?

When have you been able to find the little child in you, and to let him/her know that you, the adult, are there for him/her?

What does your little child need from you in order to feel safe, secure, and empowered?

How can you determine when the opinions and motives of others are helpful or harmful to your relationship with your partner?

What must you do to prevent a sabotage of your happiness and to develop inner trust?

Do you practice saying what you mean and meaning what you say?

How does it help you to understand that the ability to be there for yourself will be a catalyst to releasing your fears?

Have you fully committed to working on yourself? Your marriage? To letting go of fear?

How do you take responsibility for your own behavior?

What feelings about your parents and/or your childhood wounds do you project onto your partner?

What are your negative and positive expectations of your partner?

Have you tried using the practice of meditation to relieve your worries and clear your thoughts?

How does the value of trusting yourself expand your life?

How does being honest with your emotions improve your integrity and commitment?

What positive behaviors did your parents model for you?

How do you think the truth will free you?

How does living one day at a time and expressing your truth each day help create happiness?

How does living one day at a time prevent the past from re-occurring?

Why is it important for you to tend to the needs of the little child in you?

What does the little child in you need?

How do you feel when you nourish and comfort the little child in you?

How does taking the blame out of your life help you develop the habit of learning from your mistakes and correcting them?

Why do you think this habit will help you find happiness and alleviate pain?

At what times do you react to your partner the way your parents reacted to each other or the way you reacted to your parents as a child?

What is your prescription for happiness?

When you approach your relationship with positive perceptions, what becomes available to you and your partner and your marriage?

What will help you to develop confidence in yourself?

How does understanding your childhood wounds help you realize why you react as you do to your partner? What can you do to change that reaction?

When do you observe your own behavior and listen to how you respond to others?

How does eliminating blame, shame, and criticism from your life help to deepen your love?

How would forgiveness of another heal and simplify your life?

When do you observe your own behavior and listen to how you respond to others?

When have you realized that what you dislike in your partner is found within yourself?

How have you tried to solve the enigma?

What is your "vision" for your marriage?

What would the "magic" look like in your marriage?

Are you willing to trust your partner?

Are you willing to speak the truth to your partner?

Are you willing to take action?

Are you ready to take responsibility for your feelings?

Are you ready to stop blaming your spouse?

Do you realize you must help yourself first and not fear that by broaching the subject of your feelings you will lose the magic of love?

About the Author

$\mathcal{D}$r. Denkin, the host of "Catch Your Kids Doing Things Right," a four-part television series in which she taught many of her techniques to a wide audience, has been trained and certified as an Imago Relationship Therapist by Dr. Harville Hendrix, best selling author of "Getting The Love You Want" et al. She was recently honored by The University of Bridgeport with a Most Distinguished Alumni Award.

Eydie is the author of "Why Can't You Catch Me Being Good?" How to raise self-confident and well-behaved children and has embraced a spiritual quest and a personal calling to help people find their childhood triggers and help them reclaim their emotional freedom and happiness.

Her long-term marriage has survived and thrived through both partners' achieving the personal growth needed, found in each of the stages of marriage and relationship.

Relationship Magic is possible for you!

For more information, please visit us at:
www.edythedenkin.com
or call us at: 1-888-966-9445

Large Print Edition Also Available

Imago

Imago Relationships International was co-founded by Harville Hendrix PhD and Helen LaKelly Hunt PhD to help couples and individuals to create strong and fulfilling relationships. We offer the following:

- Weekend workshops based on *Getting The Love You Want* are available at many locations in the USA and internationally. Over 6,000 couples take this workshop each year.
- Over 1,000 Certified Imago Therapists are available in over 20 countries. They can guide you through the Imago process and help you achieve the relationship of your dreams.
- You can sign up at no cost for our monthly email newsletter, with stories from couples, and a look at Imago in practice.
- We have a range of audio and video programs based on Imago, including "Through Conflict to Connection", an introductory DVD showing three couples using Imago dialogue, featuring Harville Hendrix and Helen LaKelly Hunt.
- Information on training programs for mental-health professionals, coaches and educators which can help you work more effectively with couples and families
- We also offer workshops for individuals, and are introducing parenting programs

For information on these and other Imago programs please visit our website:

www.GettingTheLoveYouWant.com
Or call 1-800-729-1121

In addition you can find information about
the Imago program for religious groups by visiting
www.couplehoodasaspiritualpath.com